I SEE YOU

HOW TO BREAK FREE
FROM ABUSIVE RELATIONSHIPS
AND RECLAIM YOUR POWER:
MY STORY

NICOLE LOGIS

Copyright © 2024 Soulful Healing Hypnotherapy

All rights reserved. No part of this publication may be reproduced, stored in a retrieval system, or transmitted in any form or by any means, electronic, mechanical, photocopying, recording or otherwise, without the prior written permission from both the copyright owner and publisher.

For permission requests, email soulfulhealinghypnosis@gmail.com

Disclaimer

The content in this book, I See You, is intended for informational and educational purposes only and is not a substitute for professional advice or therapy. The author's experiences and those of others shared within these pages aim to offer insight and empowerment. Each individual's experience with trauma and abuse is unique; readers should seek professional help tailored to their circumstances.

All references to people have been anonymised, and any resemblance to real persons is coincidental. The author intends not to defame or harm but to share her story to inspire and support others.

The author and publisher disclaim any liability or responsibility for any outcomes related to using this book's information.

Published by Soulful Healing Hypnotherapy 2024
Publishing Partnership with Change Maker Press Pty Ltd

ISBN 978-1-7637927-0-8 (Paperback)

I SEE YOU

Thank you
for choosing my book.

I hope you enjoy reading my story
as much as I loved writing it.

You only get one chance in life,
Let's create your new story
together

Love Nicole xx

My First Gift to You

Thank you for purchasing I See You and taking the first step toward breaking free and reclaiming your power. Your journey is important, and I want to ensure you have all the tools and support you need.

As a gift, I invite you to download the Limitless Minds Rise Above audio program for free. This audio program is designed to deepen your experience, support your growth, empower your mind, and be an essential part of your reflection and healing as you move through the book.

Use this link or QR code to access the website: https://bit.ly/3UHfrPK. Once there, scroll down to find the Rise Above program, click on it, create your login, and enjoy your journey!

Rise Above

CONTENTS

I Can't be Broken **01**

Understanding The Unconscious Mind **13**

Understanding Trauma Bonds And Dissociation **20**

Rose-coloured Glasses **25**

Generational Abuse **31**

Understanding Control **41**

The Fox and The Rabbit **45**

The Abuser **48**

Physical Abuse **56**

Red Flags **76**

Sexual Abuse **82**

Remember Your Worth **90**

Emotional and Psychological Abuse **92**

Verbal Abuse **109**

Financial Abuse **118**

The Ten W's of Life **131**

Addicted to Hope **133**

The Power of Denial **142**

Maybe Syndrome **147**

Feeling Isolated, Lost and Alone **152**

Where There is Pain, There is Light **158**

The Power of Women in Ancient Times **170**

The Non-Negotiables **174**

'The Let It Go' Theory **177**

Finding Support in Australia – You Are Not Alone **180**

What Does a Healthy Relationship Look Like **186**

You've Got This! **197**

About the Author: Nicole Logis **203**

Let's Connect **205**

I Can't be Broken

To My Abuser,

Thank you.

Thank you for the pain, the heartache, and the struggles.

Through it all, I found my strength, the kind of strength I never knew I had. You unknowingly pushed me to discover the depths of my resilience and the woman I've become today.

It wasn't easy, and I didn't see the lessons hidden beneath the hurt for a long time. But through healing, forgiveness, and self-love, I've come to understand that every wound has made me stronger. Every scar tells the story of the woman who survived and learned to rise above what tried to break her.

I am no longer the person you tried to mould. I have become more than your hurtful words, more than the fear, and more than the person I was when we met. I've learned to trust myself again, to believe in my worth, and to set boundaries that protect my peace.

Thank you for the lessons you didn't realise you were teaching me. You showed me what love isn't, and I've learned what real love feels like, starting with the love I give myself. You showed me who I was not to be, so I've become exactly who I'm meant to be.

I've forgiven you, and in that forgiveness, I found freedom. I no longer carry the weight of our past. I've let go of the bitterness and the anger because they no longer serve me. Instead, I'm grateful for the woman I am now, strong, independent, and healed.

So, thank you—not for the hurt but for the lessons it brought. You were a chapter in my life, not my whole story.

I'm writing the rest, and it's full of hope, love, and the kind of strength that only comes from surviving what I did because I can't be broken.

Nicole xx

This is for the beautiful, strong, independent, empowering woman reading this.

You are the director of your movie, and you my beautiful soul are the star.

I See You, I Hear You, I Get You.

YOU ARE NOT ALONE. ALWAYS REMEMBER, YOU ARE ENOUGH.

When I began writing this book, finding the correct title took me some time. Then it hit me—*I See You.* The power of those words resonated deeply. You see, my dear reader, for so long-you may have felt invisible, unheard, and unseen by those who should have cared for you. *I See You* is more than just a title. It's a message, a reflection of the journey you've been on and the one I've walked myself.

I See You is about finally being recognised for who you are—not through the lens of an abuser, but through the clarity of your own eyes. It's about seeing yourself as the worthy, resilient person you truly are.

There's another layer to *I See You* as well. It's about taking off those rose-coloured glasses and seeing the abuse, the abuser, and the relationship for what they really are.

You may have overlooked the red flags for so long, excused the behaviour, and told yourself things weren't as bad as they seemed. *I See You* means you're now ready to see the truth, even if it's painful. It's about seeing the abuser for who they really are—someone who manipulated, controlled, and betrayed you. It's about seeing the reality of the situation, without the denial or wishful thinking, and finally understanding the toxic, damaging cycle you were caught in.

I wrote this book because, had I not changed my life, I would have spiralled into a place I couldn't escape. By sharing my story, I hope to resonate with anyone feeling stuck, numb or lost. I see you, and I hope this book helps you see yourself, too.

If you're reading this, a part of you is ready to break free. Maybe you're questioning everything, wondering how you got here, and looking for a way out of the hurt, self-doubt, and confusion.

Here's what I've learned: Trauma doesn't just leave scars; it fundamentally shifts who we are at our core. The journey isn't about returning to who we once were—it's about becoming who we are truly meant to be. Many individuals complete traditional trauma treatment only to ask, "What now?" They may feel somewhat better but yearn for their former selves, unaware that this desire to return to the past and reclaim an old identity can become a trap. We can't go back. But we can grow forward.

How dare they speak to us like we are nothing? Who do they think they are to treat us this way? They are not gods, not our fathers, and we are not their children. We are women with our own minds, our own choices, and an undeniable right to live free from fear and control. They are nothing more than bullies, lashing out because they can't bear the weight of their own pain, projecting their hurt onto us. They despise our strength, so they try to weaken us, knowing we are empaths who instinctively give to help, even at the cost of our power.

But no more. This is not on. We need to ask ourselves—who helps *us*? Who makes *us* stand strong? Stop bending for those who thrive on breaking us.

We are more than their projections, more than the bruises they leave behind, whether seen or unseen. We are resilient, we are fierce, and it's time we stand tall for ourselves and each other. No one will silence us anymore. We are here to claim our worth, our voice, and our right to live free and unbreakable.

I do see you because I've been there too. I've been made to sleep on the floor while heavily pregnant, being punched in the dark so I wouldn't see it coming. I have faced every horror you can imagine, and yet, I'm still standing.

As I write these words, the fire in my belly burns fiercely to see every woman rise. This is our time to stand tall, know our worth, and take back what has always been ours: our freedom, strength, and power.

I thank God every day that my rose-coloured glasses were removed, and I could see the relationship for what it truly was: a lie, a facade. It still breaks my heart to know I gave two decades to this man, pouring so much of myself into something that wasn't real.

Picking up the pieces hasn't been easy, but there is a light, my dear reader. Even if you only see darkness now, know that strength, power, and growth await you on the other side. As you heal, you'll see their weakness and see them for who they are, and as you change and transform, you'll reclaim the strength they tried to take from you.

Hypnotherapy was my lifeline and one of the most powerful tools in my healing journey, and I'll discuss it throughout the book. It made a real difference for me, and while I don't want anyone to feel pressured to try it, it's a big part of my story and something I believe in.

My dear reader, please know this. As you read through these pages, you'll find the stories of my clients who, like you, have struggled to break free from trauma bonds and the painful cycle of abuse.

In these chapters, I dive into the different forms of abuse—physical, emotional, verbal, psychological, and financial—because I believe it's essential for women to recognise these signs.

From my experience working with clients, many were unaware of the abuse they were enduring, often seeing their situation through rose-coloured glasses, which in turn is the illusion of denial.

> *I want you to know you are not alone,*
> *and I get you.*
> *I have been there, and it's okay.*

At 50 years of age, I found my purpose: going through a consistent cycle of making up and breaking up whilst being on my own as a single mother, trying to bring up my children, struggling financially and with my mental health, and even though we lived apart the gaslighting, the breadcrumbs, the love bombing and broken promises I held onto, made me feel like I was going crazy and it felt like I was on this roller coaster ride that never ended until the day I decided to get off.

It wasn't easy. I was so trauma-bonded to this man and under the illusion of this distorted love.

> *You see, my dear reader,*
> *I have been where you are multiple*
> *times.*

Picking up the pieces and peeling back the layers of my past was hard work. Those layers ran deep, rooted in the dysfunction and lack of love I witnessed growing up. What I thought was normal was far from it. Seeing the truth from the outside looking in revealed the distortion. The hardest part of healing was learning to love myself.

After reading *I See You*, I want you to feel truly seen and heard. I want you to understand that the version of yourself they tried to create—the one they want you to believe you are—is not who you truly are. You were not made by their words, actions, or control.

Inside, you hold the power to redefine yourself and change your life. No matter how trapped you may feel, know that you possess a strength more significant than you realise, a courage that's been waiting to rise. You can break free, you can heal, and you can write a new chapter in your life - one that reflects who *you* really are.

If I can do it, you can too. It's time to stop believing in "better the devil you know." I understand the fear—it's overwhelming, the fear of the unknown, the fear of what the future holds without them. But let me ask you, is it truly better to stay where you are, feeling depleted, living for someone else instead of for yourself?

Stop living in denial! Stop believing their words, stop listening to the lies that keep you doubting yourself, accept less, and live on the breadcrumbs they throw your way. You deserve so much more.

Freedom. What a beautiful word. Freedom to speak your truth, wear what you want, make choices that are yours alone, and leave the dishes in the sink if that's what you want. This is *your* time, my dear reader. It's time to stop surviving for them and start *living* for you.

> ### *'You are the shining light; allow yourself to be seen because you are a Queen.'*

I am determined to be the voice for every woman who has endured an abusive relationship.

Enough is enough!

We have been mistreated for far too long, and I refuse to stay silent any longer.

This is your time to rise, my dear reader. You chose this book for a reason. Now, let's reclaim your worth and know, beyond a shadow of a doubt, that you deserve a life of love, freedom, and immense happiness.

The world is waiting for you to take that step, and I am here, walking beside you.

Now, my dear reader, before we go further, I want to prepare you for what's to come. I share specific examples of the abuse I endured. It's my intention to be open and real so that I can reach and support women who need to see that they are not alone.

However, if you are sensitive to these topics or feel triggered, please be mindful of your emotional well-being as you read. Take breaks when needed, and remember that your safety and peace come first.

I See You, I've Got You,

Nicole xx

"Dancing with Shadows"

In the spotlight's glow, they appear so divine,

Abusers dance, their egos in line.

Charisma like music, their smiles so bright,

But beware of the shadows they cast in the light.

Their mesmerising dance draws you in with charm and puts you in a trance.

But their self-absorbed waltz, a toxic embrace,

Leaves hearts shattered and minds in a chase.

Their world is a stage where empathy is amiss,

A reel of manipulation, a dance of emotional abyss.

A partner to their performance, you unknowingly become,

In their grand production, a puppet, undone.

Gaslighting twists reality, truth's threads they weave,

In this reel of deception, it's hard to perceive.

You question your sanity as they rewrite the script,
Their self-centred ego is a power they grip.
But within their grasp, strength will find its rise,
Breaking free from their hold, unveiling the lies.
The reel now fades as the truth takes its stance,
We learn to detect the abusers' dance.
Empowered by knowledge, we reclaim our might,
No longer blinded by their deceptive light.
Remember, dear dancer, the reel can be stopped,
Break free from their spell; let self-love be your plot.
In the aftermath of healing, we reclaim our worth,
No longer entrapped by the abusers' curse.

Nicole Logis

Understanding The Unconscious Mind

> "My past does not define my future; I create my path. I am enough, just as I am, embracing my unique worth. I am worthy of love, respect, and kindness and step forward confidently and strongly."

My dear reader, as I guide you through each step of the book, I want you to feel the transformation and healing I experienced while writing it. This journey is one of hope and optimism, and I am here to guide you through it.

When I first began exploring the subconscious mind, I started to understand so much about myself—why

I acted the way I did, made the choices I did, and how my behaviours seemed almost automatic. I realised how deeply we can mirror the people we're closest to, especially in relationships. Without knowing it, we pick up on their habits, reactions, and ways of seeing the world.

This understanding was an eye-opener, helping me see that so much of what I thought was "just me" was actually shaped by my subconscious and my relationships. This awareness was the first step toward real change, and I hope sharing it with you offers the same kind of clarity and insight.

We are born into this world as pure, innocent souls, and most of us are already traumatised whilst in the womb. So, we already hold onto the emotions of what our mothers carried during the pregnancy. It seems we repeat history.

As newborns, our minds are open and receptive to the world like blank canvases. From the moment we enter this world until age seven, we are in a highly impressionable state. Our subconscious mind absorbs everything we experience during these years, especially from our family environment.

In these early years, we see and internalise the dynamics of our family life. If we grow up in a dysfunctional family where love and security are overshadowed by conflict, neglect, or abuse, these negative patterns seep into our subconscious mind. We learn what relationships look like from our parents or caregivers, shaping our understanding of what is expected and acceptable. This, my dear reader, is where the distortion of love begins. I remember everything from age four onward, and I will discuss this further in the book.

By the time we reach the age of seven, the foundation of our subconscious mind is primarily set. The beliefs and patterns formed during these early years begin to solidify. If we have witnessed unhealthy relationships, we might subconsciously believe that this is what we deserve or that this is how love should be. These deep-seated beliefs can profoundly influence our choices and behaviours, often without realising it.

As we grow older, these dysfunctional patterns and beliefs guide our actions and our choices in life, which often lead us into relationships that mirror the dysfunction we experienced in our early years. Unfortunately, we are attracted and drawn to partners who replicate the dynamics of our family. This would more than likely be the representation of your father but also your mother; for me, it was both, extending a cycle of abuse and dysfunction.

Understanding this pattern and looking outward is the first step towards breaking the generational cycle. By recognising the impact of our early experiences on our subconscious mind, we can begin the journey of healing and transformation.

Through my trauma healing program and using modalities like HypnoQi, which combines hypnotherapy and Reiki, we can reprogram the subconscious mind, release old patterns, and build new, healthier beliefs about ourselves and our relationships. This unique approach helps balance and clear negative energy from the body, allowing you to move forward with renewed strength and empowerment.

This, my dear reader, is the transformation of *MIND, BODY AND SOUL*. This empowers us to create a future free from the shadows of our past, where we can experience genuine love, respect, and fulfilment. And this, my dear reader, is why I chose to become a hypnotherapist and Reiki Master to help women like yourself change their subconscious mind, remove those limiting beliefs of fear of abandonment, feeling alone, not good enough, and the list goes on. Hypnotherapy and Reiki are like creating magic. It removes all your triggers and helps you *FEEL* again! No more feeling numb! You gain clarity and feel the shift!

I know you are questioning right now. Does this work? It bloody does!!! Trust me, by changing your subconscious mind and healing from the inside out, you view your life differently. The more you change, the more toxic fleas (these are the takers) start dropping off because they don't want to see the best out of you; they want to keep you down. So! Let's change and remove those fleas!!!!

Have you ever truly been asked what you want? I remember the first time someone asked me that question, and I was left speechless. After a lifetime of being controlled, from childhood to my partner, I didn't know how to think for myself. I was always told what to do and never asked what I wanted. So, I invite you now to take a moment and ask yourself: *What do you want?*

Take a piece of paper and write down everything that comes to mind. Be honest. Are these goals realistic? If they are, then go for them, girl! You deserve to pursue your dreams, however big or small. If some goals seem out of reach right now, don't remove them—acknowledge them, and know that every step forward gets you closer to reclaiming your power and living life on your terms.

I now know what I want, and that is for you to know I am right beside you, reading this book with you. You are not alone. I am here with you always.

So, my beautiful soul, let us break this generational cycle together because we deserve a loving relationship, someone who adores us and places us on a pedestal. But before we enter this wonderful loving relationship, we must learn to have a loving relationship with ourselves and put ourselves on a pedestal, stop people pleasing, learn to say no, make ourselves a priority, dance, laugh, feel again and know what you want! How exhilarating is that feeling! Feel it, breathe it in, imagine it; let's create this new story for you. We only get one life, One Chance. Let's do this!

I've got you _{xx}

My Gift

Today, dear reader, if you haven't already, I invite you to visit the Limitless Minds website to access the Rise Above audio program for free. Use this link: https://bit.ly/3UHfrPK, then scroll down to find the program. Click on Rise Above, create your login, and start listening!

This audio emphasises self-affirmation, guiding you to declare your worthiness and resilience. It culminates in a powerful moment of self-recognition, where you stand firm in your identity and feel a surge of energy and confidence.

Understanding Trauma Bonds And Dissociation

"I am worthy of love and respect. I choose to honour my strength and release what no longer serves me. I am healing, I am growing, and I am free."

Before beginning my story, my dear reader, you must understand the trauma bond and the cycle. As you read my story, you will ask yourself, why did I keep going back? I need you to know I was stuck on the roller coaster ride and didn't know how to get off; I knew the cycle; I knew I didn't deserve this, but the fear of leaving and the distorted love I had for my abuser was intense.

I just kept thinking, "Better the devil you know; he's the father to my kids", which meant in my distorted mind that he could do anything he liked to me. You see when you're in an abusive relationship, it can be incredibly confusing and heartbreaking not only to yourself but for the people who care about you, especially your children, to watch you keep going back to someone who hurts you multiple times.

To help you understand this, we must discuss two crucial things: the trauma bond and how the subconscious mind protects us by dissociation. These are ways your mind tries to protect you, even though they can end up keeping you trapped in a cycle of abuse. When you forgive them and instantly forget what they have done, this is your dissociation.

Trauma bonding is a powerful emotional attachment that forms between you and your abuser. It's not just any bond; it strengthens when you are hurt and then shown moments of kindness or love (breadcrumbs). This cycle of pain, followed by affection, creates a deep connection that's hard to break. Crazy right? But it's bloody true.

I'll give an example: One day, they are so cruel, putting you down, calling you names, making you feel worthless. But the next day, they apologise, tell you they love you, and show you attention. In those moments of kindness, your mind clings to the hope that things will improve;

maybe this time, they mean it. This hope is what creates the trauma bond. The relationship is black and white, with no grey.

Your brain starts associating the moments of love and kindness with relief from the pain. You begin to believe that things will change if you try harder if you're more patient or understanding. But the truth is, this cycle keeps repeating, and each time it does, the bond gets more substantial, making it harder to leave.

Now, dissociation, which I find fascinating, is how our subconscious mind protects us from the pain of abuse. When the hurt becomes too much, your subconscious mind might "switch off" specific memories or emotions. This is your brain's way of creating distance between you and the trauma so you can survive it.

The subconscious mind is so powerful that it helps you forget some of the worst moments. You might feel like you're watching your life from the outside as if it's happening to someone else.

This detachment can make it easier to stay in the relationship because your mind isn't fully processing how bad things are.

But while dissociation helps you cope, it also keeps you stuck. By not fully acknowledging the abuse, it becomes easier to forgive, excuse your partner's behaviour, and stay in the cycle. It's like your mind is shielding you from the reality of the situation, but in doing so, it's also keeping you from breaking free.

Understanding trauma bonding and dissociation is the first step toward breaking free from the cycle of abuse. It's important to know that these are natural responses. Your subconscious mind is trying to protect you. But to truly heal and move forward, you must recognise and work to overcome these patterns. So, once again, you can overcome this through the combination of Hypnotherapy, Timeline Therapy and Reiki, restoring and healing the mind, body and soul and listening to the Hypno-App Limitless Minds Hypnotherapy just like I did! When you are hurting and want to jump off the ride, HypnoQ works like magic. It instantly changes the subconscious mind and helps you gain clarity and strength.

Remember, my beautiful soul, you deserve a relationship where love doesn't hurt.

Recognising the bond that keeps you tied to your abuser and the ways your mind might be distancing you from the pain is crucial in finding the strength to leave and stay away. It's a difficult journey, but understanding these concepts can help you see the situation more clearly and empower you to take the steps needed to move into the next chapter of your life.

Unfortunately, these abusers know which buttons to press to get us hooked back into the cycle. Take away a toy, and the little boy cries. Take away a relationship that is convenient to him, he cries. And yes, my dear reader, we are only a convenience to them; the word 'love' does not exist in their vocabulary. They only know the word 'use'. Remember this the next time the abuser says I love you when he means I use you.

Love isn't telling your abuser that he needs to change to keep you; love is an honest man changing on his own because he can't imagine life without you. Let us choose to be loved the right way, not the wrong. Remember your worth, and we are bloody worth it!!

I've got you $_{xx}$

Rose-coloured Glasses

> "I choose to remove the rose-coloured glasses and see the truth. I embrace clarity, trust my intuition, and honour my strength. I deserve to see the world as it is, not as I wish it to be. With open eyes and a brave heart, I reclaim my power and reality."

My dear reader, I lived in a world where it felt like I wore a pair of rose-coloured glasses that softened the harshness of my reality, obscuring the red flags and masking the true nature of my relationship.

These glasses weren't just a metaphor; they were my shield. I remember convincing myself that the yelling was just stress, that the isolation from friends was protection, and that the bruises were accidents. Each justification added another layer to those tinted lenses, allowing me to survive the daily emotional turmoil by making myself believe that things weren't as bad as they seemed.

There were moments when I would see glimpses of the truth, like when I found myself apologising for his outbursts or when he covered my mouth during labour because I was embarrassing him. This took away every ounce of my dignity. But the rose-coloured glasses would slip back into place, allowing me to ignore reality, use my famous words, whatever doesn't matter, and endure the suffocating silence that followed his cruelty.

These glasses, this self-deception, became my way to cope, to hold onto the hope that things could change. But deep down, I knew—no matter how much I wanted to deny it—that the illusion was my cage. It was only when I finally took off those glasses, shattered by the undeniable truth, that I began to see clearly and reclaim my strength.

I lived in a world where it was as if I wore a pair of rose-coloured glasses that softened the harshness of my reality, obscuring the red flags and masking the true nature of my relationship. These glasses were not just a metaphor. They were my defence mechanism, a way to survive the daily emotional turmoil by convincing myself that things weren't as bad as they seemed.

Through those lenses, the moments of kindness were magnified, and the hurtful words were minimised. I saw the potential of what could be rather than the painful reality of what was. Each time I was hurt, I told myself it was just a misunderstanding, that love would conquer all, and that things would eventually change. The glasses made me believe that my passion was genuine and mutual and that everything would be okay if I just held on a little longer.

But there came a day when those glasses began to crack. Perhaps it was a moment of clarity, a small crack in the facade that let reality seep through. Maybe it was the realisation that no amount of love could justify the pain I was enduring. Or perhaps it was simply exhaustion from pretending, making excuses, trying to force a happy ending in a story that was never meant to be.

When those glasses finally shattered, I was left spinning. The shock was overwhelming, like stepping out of a dream into a nightmare. Everything that had been obscured before was suddenly in sharp focus, and the reality I saw was nothing like the fantasy I had clung to. The love I thought I had was a mirage, and the person I believed in was a stranger—someone who had caused me more pain than I had ever acknowledged.

In that moment of clarity, the weight of the truth crashed down on me. I saw the manipulation, the control, the subtle ways I had been diminished and broken down. I saw how my self-worth had been depleted and worn away, how I had become a shadow of who I once was. The rose-coloured glasses had protected me from this truth, but they had also trapped me in a cycle of denial and pain.

The shock of removing those glasses was enormous. It was like waking up from a deep sleep, disoriented and struggling to make sense of the world around me. I questioned everything—how could I have been so blind? How had I let things get so bad? Why didn't I see the truth sooner?

But as painful as that shock was, it was also liberating. Without the glasses, I could finally see clearly. I could see the relationship for what it was—a toxic, abusive cycle that had been disguised as love. And in that clarity, I found the strength to walk away, begin the healing process, and reclaim my power.

The journey of taking off those rose-coloured glasses was not easy. It required facing painful truths, confronting my denial, and mourning the loss of the fantasy I had believed in for so long. But it was a necessary step—a step towards freedom, towards self-love, and towards a life that was no longer defined by someone else's abuse.

In the end, the shock of reality was a gift. It was the wake-up call to break free, stop making excuses, and start living for myself. As I moved forward, I promised never to wear those glasses again. I would face the world with my eyes wide open, ready to see the truth, no matter how uncomfortable it might be.

Only by seeing the truth can we truly heal. Only in facing reality can we find the strength to change our lives. Only by taking off those rose-coloured glasses can we finally see the world as it is and begin to create the life we deserve.

I've got you _{xx}

My Gift

Today, dear reader, I was hoping you could identify your rose-coloured glasses and reflect on the moments in your relationship where you may have ignored their behaviour and excused their actions.

Generational Abuse

> "I am the one who breaks the cycle. I release the pain, fear, and patterns passed down through generations. I choose healing, love, and peace for myself and those who come after me. The chains of generational trauma end with me. I am free, I am strong, and I am creating a new legacy of love, empowerment, and resilience."

***Definition of Generational Abuse:** Generational abuse, also known as intergenerational abuse, refers to patterns of abusive behaviour that are passed down from one generation to the next within families. This cycle can involve physical, emotional, sexual, or psychological abuse, and it often perpetuates because children who grow up in abusive environments may come to view such behaviour as normal* *or acceptable. They may then repeat these patterns in their relationships and with their children.*

And this, my dear reader, is how the cycle begins.

I was born in Sydney, Australia, and lived in Rockdale. I am of Greek descent but wasn't raised in the strict Greek culture. I have a brother and a sister, and I am the eldest, which meant I had to lead by example. We lived comfortably and never went without. I would consider myself the 'Black Sheep' of the family.

Growing up, I was always the fat child. My mother, who took immense pride in her appearance, couldn't understand why her daughter was overweight. She took me to doctors, hoping to find an answer, but all it did was intensify the shame I felt about myself. She would make fun of my body, comparing my big ass to the back of a bus, saying if I kept eating, it would only get bigger. The constant put-downs were relentless, and there were few clothes for bigger girls back then, so my mother would make my clothes. This only added to my feelings of isolation and embarrassment; in her defence, she thought that by putting me down, I would do something about my weight, but it didn't.

To make matters worse, my father would sometimes use me as a pawn in his battles with my mother. In moments of rage, he would claim that I wasn't his child, a cruel tactic designed to hurt her. Their fights were frequent and intense, and often, they would reach out to me, pulling me into their conflicts and using me as a tool to vent their frustrations.

I felt like an outsider in my own family; I wasn't seen or heard; I was just controlled and moulded to fit their expectations and to serve as an outlet for their anger and disappointment.

By the age of 15, I tried to take my life. I look back now and know that I had reached a dark time in my life when I just wanted to be seen!

Hello! I am a human being with feelings!

I went to counselling, and of course, my father chose not to come because he wasn't the problem; I was. Let's be honest: I was the problem, and that's how I felt.

When I reached 18, I finally looked at myself in the mirror and decided that was it. I was going on a diet, so I went to Weight Watchers and the weight wasn't coming off quickly, so I decided to start vomiting.

I was looking great and had lost weight, but internally, I was still the fat girl. I struggled and, till now, still struggle with body dysmorphia, and the binge eating and vomiting lasted for many years. That became an addiction; the more I felt I was losing control, dealing with stress, or looking at myself in the mirror, thinking I was fat, which I wasn't, the more I vomited. This was my way of dealing with control. I was in control of my eating; weird, hey, I know, but it was a compulsion of mine. To this day, I look back at photos and say wow, I was very slim; I know where my head space was then.

Now that I have grown and healed, I realise my parents didn't know any better. They were kids raising kids without guidance from their parents, caught in a cycle passed down to us. They didn't know how to communicate respectfully and compassionately, trying to understand at least what was happening. They just stayed in blame and judged. Their love was conditional, not unconditional.

Consistent obligations felt like a game that never ended if I hurt them. Trying to please them was exhausting when I only wanted validation and love; I was craving love.

My father, despite his flaws, was a great provider. However, he wasn't there emotionally. My mother, overwhelmed by her unhappiness, directed all her anger and frustration at me. I bore the brunt of her emotional outbursts, and nothing I did could ever make her happy. Nothing was ever good enough.

I looked up to my father. He was my support, my safe place. Whenever my mother would speak badly to me, my father would stick up for me. I put him on a pedestal, seeing him as my protector, even though I also watched him abuse my mother. These conflicting feelings—seeing my father as both an abuser and a saviour created a confusing mix of emotions that I struggled to understand.

Throughout my childhood and even up until today, my parents have always blamed others for any mishap in the family. It was always someone else's fault, never theirs. They never took a moment to look at themselves and realise that the problems often stemmed from their actions and choices, not from others. This refusal to accept responsibility only enabled the cycle of dysfunction and pain.

Unfortunately, my mother was not easy to turn to for support, as she was quite an opinionated woman and controlling in so many ways. She didn't like me because I reminded her of my father. I was close to my dad, but a daughter can only say so much to her father. I had to figure everything out on my own. I needed a mother, and I yearned for her to be my best friend and see me for who I was, not the version she created, but the love and nurturing support were never there. Instead, I relied on my close friends for the support I craved, and I am so grateful that those friends are still in my life today.

I was told I needed to finish school which I hated; I wanted to be a hairdresser, I was told that I was going to be a paralegal, which my mother worked hard to get me through business college, but I didn't want to go, so I went feeling obligated, I was told what to wear and as my mother said, "Lucky you're fat cause you would dress like a slut". I was told all my growing years what I should become, not what I wanted.

Because I was so controlled mentally, I was vulnerable to the world and thought everyone was friendly. You judge everyone through yourself and think the world is like you, but they are not, and at 20, I met my abuser.

I recently reconnected with my family. Before this, they chose to cut ties with me because they were tired of the cycle I was in with my children's father. They couldn't understand the cycle, nor did they want to acknowledge it. They treated me like a criminal. While they did try to guide me, their approach was so dysfunctional that it only confused me and made things worse, especially while I was in an abusive relationship. They didn't know how to support me and how they could help when they weren't supported in their childhood. Whatever they experienced growing up, they brought into our family home.

The values and beliefs instilled in us as children are powerful. Watching my mother be mistreated yet stay in the marriage taught me that family values meant enduring pain and suffering. I learned that we don't leave; we put up with it. This belief became deeply ingrained, shaping my understanding of relationships and self-worth.

Looking from the outside in, I realise how these experiences impacted me. The generational cycle of abuse is a vicious cycle passed down through behaviours and beliefs that we absorb as children. Understanding this cycle is the first step towards breaking free, and guess what? I broke the bloody cycle! It took a while, but I did it.

As I see my children grow, they have all ended up in beautiful relationships, one that I now long for. I see how they have learnt through my mistakes, and watching my son and his daughter together is the most beautiful and exhilarating feeling I have ever encountered.

I cry writing this as so many memories rush by. My kids were unfortunately dealt a tough life, and breaking the generational pattern is even more challenging. But they did it, and I am so bloody proud of them.

WE DID IT.

The generational cycle is severed, and we are all free.

If you're searching for the one person who can and will change your life, look in the mirror

I want to share with you, my dear reader, the first time I realised how strong family values and beliefs are. I learnt this through my experience with my beautiful client, whom we will call Sophia.

Sophia grew up in a household where abuse was disguised as discipline and control. Her parents had strong family values, which, unfortunately, included suffering for family unity. She was always taught that leaving was never an option, and this belief kept her trapped in an abusive relationship for years.

When Sophia came to me, she was emotionally exhausted and felt completely depleted of self-worth. We began her healing journey with HypnoQi. Through hypnotherapy, we accessed her subconscious mind to resolve the deep-seated beliefs that were keeping her in the cycle of abuse. Timeline therapy allowed her to revisit and heal past traumas, helping her see her experiences from a new perspective. Reiki provided the energetic healing she needed to restore balance and peace within herself.

After several sessions, Sophia started feeling light and confident. She clarified her self-worth and realised that she deserved love and respect. The strong family values she once held began to shift as she understood the importance of breaking free from toxic patterns.

Today, Sophia is in a loving relationship with a wonderful man and just had her first child. She is an inspiration to me, and as Sophia grew, I found that the more she connected with herself, loved herself, and became that better version of herself, the more she attracted love and the love of her life, and she has never been happier. I will always remember Sophia.

My Gift

Today, dear reader, I want you to go out into nature, go to a park or the beach, take your shoes off and ground yourself. No phone! Look around and listen to the ocean or the people around you. Enjoy the time, and let's enjoy Mother Earth and what she gives us.

The simple things in life are free; breathe.

I've got you xx

Understanding Control

> "I reclaim my power. I am free to make my own choices, and I release the grip of control. I am worthy of love, respect, and freedom."

Definition of Control: *In an abusive relationship, control refers to one partner's efforts to dominate the other through manipulation, coercion, or intimidation. It often involves restricting the victim's independence, freedom, or choices, making them feel powerless. The abuser may control aspects of the victim's life, such as finances, communication, social interactions, and even emotions, often using fear, guilt, or threats to maintain dominance. This control keeps the victim dependent and trapped in the relationship, reinforcing the cycle of abuse.*

Control in an abusive relationship is like an invisible chain, binding you in ways that may not always be obvious at first. It's about power—the abuser's need to dominate every aspect of your life, often leaving you feeling helpless, confused, and trapped. Control isn't just physical. It can be emotional, verbal, financial, or psychological—each form slowly eroding your sense of self and freedom.

As you read through this book, you'll see how control shows up in many forms:

- **Physical Control:** Using physical force or the threat of violence to make you feel powerless.

- **Emotional Control:** Undermining your confidence, making you doubt your worth, using guilt or manipulation to keep you dependent.

- **Verbal Control:** Using words as weapons, belittling you, making you feel small, or twisting your reality until you start to question yourself.

- **Psychological Control:** Gaslighting, manipulating your mind to believe that everything is your fault or that you are the one who needs to change.

- **Financial Control:** Controlling money, limiting your access to resources, or making financial decisions without you makes you dependent, so you feel you *can't leave.*

Throughout the chapters, you'll see how control starts as something seemingly harmless but grows into something that dictates every part of your life as it did mine.

Control is the abuser's way of maintaining power, and it's what keeps the cycle of abuse alive.

It's important to understand that no matter what form it takes, control is abuse. It's about stripping you of your independence, your voice, and your choices.

My Gift

Today, dear reader, at the end of each day for a week, write down one decision you made that reflects your choice and is not influenced by anyone else. This could be something small, like deciding what you want for dinner, or something bigger, like choosing how to spend your time. This will reinforce your sense of independence.

The Fox and The Rabbit

Before we start our chapters on abuse, I want you to know that understanding the dynamics of abuse is crucial. The analogy I use to describe the cycle with abusers is that of the fox (the abuser) and the rabbit (you).

This powerful metaphor has resonated with countless women and even with my abuser when I explained it. It paints a clear picture of how an abuser operates and how you, the survivor, are caught in this relentless cycle. I hope this analogy helps you see the patterns, recognise the traps, and understand that breaking free is not just possible—it's essential for taking back your power.

Foxes are known for being sneaky and clever predators. When I looked up how they hunt rabbits, the similarities to abusive relationships became crystal clear. Here's how it works:

The fox has sharp senses. It can detect the rabbit long before it knows it's being watched. Once the fox spots its prey, it slowly creeps closer, taking time and listening for movement. Then, when it's ready, the fox pounces. But instead of finishing the rabbit off, it plays with it. The fox lets the rabbit run, then chases it down again, over and over.

It's not about killing the rabbit right away. No, the fox isn't done playing. The rabbit grows tired, weak, and confused, but the fox keeps the game going, withholding anything that could ease the rabbit's fear, just like an abuser withholds love and affection, keeping you exactly where they want you.

Each time the rabbit runs, it gets slower and weaker, but the fox keeps it alive just long enough to start the game all over again. The rabbit wants to give up, but the fox won't allow it. The game isn't over yet. It's a cruel cycle of control, manipulation, and survival.

So, what happens to the rabbit in the end?

That's up to the rabbit, and that's where the power lies. Does the rabbit gather enough strength to run one last time while the fox isn't paying attention? Or does it finally give up?

In this story, the rabbit finds its strength. It carefully plans its escape, waiting for the fox to get distracted, and then runs. The fox gives chase but, in the end, lets the rabbit go because now the fox is ready to play with another.

And just like that, the rabbit is finally free.

Now, my dear reader, think about yourself as that rabbit. Imagine what it would feel like to break free from that endless, exhausting game finally. You've been chased, worn down, and kept in fear, but the strength to escape has always been inside you. You can run one last time to break free and leave the fox behind. It's your life, and you have the power to take it back.

The choice is yours.

I've got you ₓₓ

The Abuser

> "I release the hold you had on me. Your actions do not define me. I reclaim my power, my voice, and my worth. I am free."

Before we begin our journey together, I would like to leave you with a clear description of who the abuser is and how they trap us into this trauma-bonded cycle.

Definition of a Narcissist: *A narcissist is someone with Narcissistic Personality Disorder (NPD), a mental condition characterised by a pervasive pattern of grandiosity, a need for admiration, and a lack of empathy for others. Narcissists often have an inflated sense of their importance and believe they are superior to others. They may exploit or manipulate those around them maintain their self-image and fulfil their needs, often displaying entitlement and arrogance. In relationships, a narcissist* *may be controlling, dismissive of their partner's feelings, and incapable of genuine emotional connection.*

Definition of Borderline Personality Disorder (BPD):
Borderline Personality Disorder (BPD) is a mental health condition characterised by intense emotions, unstable relationships, a distorted self-image, and a fear of abandonment. Individuals with BPD often experience mood swings, impulsive behaviours, and a chronic sense of emptiness. Relationships with someone who has BPD can be tumultuous due to their fear of rejection and tendency to oscillate between idealising and devaluing their partners. This disorder often leads to intense, unstable relationships where the individual struggles with maintaining a consistent sense of identity and emotional stability.

As a therapist, I have worked with countless women who have been trauma-bonded to their abusers. Time and time again, as I listen to their stories, I am struck by the unsettling familiarity of the descriptions they provide. It's as if they all come from or have read the same book despite their different backgrounds; they all show the same characteristics, driven by the same dark motivations.

It amazes me how every story begins the same way, with the abusers presenting themselves as charming and charismatic individuals. On the surface, they appear confident, attentive, fun and even loving. This is how they draw us in, creating a façade to win our trust and affection. But beneath this mask lies a person driven by insecurity and unresolved pain. They study our likes, dislikes, dreams, and fears, mirroring us to create the illusion that we are a perfect match. This manipulation is the first step in their strategy to control and dominate us.

At the core of an abuser's behaviour is their generational trauma. Often, they have experienced abuse themselves, whether emotional, physical, or psychological. This trauma becomes ingrained in them, shaping how they view the world and distorting their sense of self-worth. They carry this pain and stuck beliefs into adulthood, unable to heal; instead, they project it onto others. This instability drives them to manipulate and control those around them to avoid facing their emotional wounds. They are intelligent and skilled and can quickly identify our strengths and vulnerabilities. Remember the fox and the rabbit analogy. This is it. They are hunters like the fox and know which rabbit they want. They often target strong, independent individuals because they see these qualities as challenging and see qualities in us that they lack, attracting them to us and enraging them simultaneously.

By mirroring our personality and values, they create a false sense of connection, making us believe we have found our soul mate and someone who truly understands and supports us. This deception makes the betrayal even more devastating. Their goal is not to build us up but to break us down and diminish the light they see in us. They will pretend to share our interests, values, and goals, all to gain our trust. They tell us what we want to hear, agree with our opinions, and pretend to support our passions. This mirroring is a powerful manipulation tool because it disarms you, making you more vulnerable to their control. Once they've established this connection, they use it to subtly influence your decisions and behaviours, steering you in directions that serve their needs, not yours.

My dear reader, have you noticed that the abuser will never praise us, and if they do, it is on a rare occasion and often followed by criticism or making us feel worthless and belittling us? They create a constant state of anxiety and self-doubt, ensuring that we feel so inadequate and dependent on them. In the beginning, the abuser may seem incredibly supportive, cheering on our dreams and ambitions. But this support is conditional and temporary. As we begin to achieve our goals, the abuser's support diminishes. They belittle our successes or make us feel guilty for pursuing our happiness. Their initial encouragement was never genuine; it was a means to gain your trust and control your future decisions.

They declare their love, commitment, and future plans with us, intending to keep us hooked. Unfortunately, these are what we call broken promises. Instead, they act to string us along, giving us hope that things will get better while they continue to manipulate and betray us.

An abuser's life is often built on lies. They are compulsive liars. They lie about their feelings, their intentions, and their past. They will tell you they love what you love, hate what you hate, and want what you want. But as time goes on, the truth starts to unravel. The things they once pretended to enjoy with you will suddenly become sources of conflict. Their lies contradict each other, creating confusion and doubt in our minds.

As the relationship progresses, it doesn't take too long before they show their true colours. The mirroring fades, and the broken promises become more frequent. They betray our trust in small ways at first by cancelling plans, breaking commitments, or being inconsistent in their words and actions.

Over time, these small betrayals escalate into larger ones, leaving you confused, hurt, and betrayed. The person you thought you knew seems to disappear, replaced by someone who constantly lets you down. The cruelty becomes more frequent. The abuser starts to isolate you, cutting you off from support systems, friends, and family. They eventually instil fear and confusion, making you question your reality. This isolation strengthens the abuser's control and weakens our resistance.

One of the most devastating aspects of being in an abusive relationship is the constant breaking of trust. The abuser's lies, broken promises, and betrayal create a cycle of hope and disappointment. We find ourselves holding onto the good moments, hoping the person who once seemed perfect will return. But the reality is that the abuser's actions are deliberate and calculated. They thrive on keeping us off balance, watching us struggle, breaking us down and depleting our self-worth to make us feel like we cannot survive without them.

You will find that abusers fear being abandoned or rejected because, deep down, they believe they are unworthy of love. This fear drives them to control us, ensuring that we remain dependent and too broken to leave.

In the end, the abuser is their own worst enemy. They destroy relationships and push away the very people they claim to love. They live in constant inner turmoil, projecting their pain onto others in a desperate attempt to avoid facing it themselves.

Now, my dear reader, this description of the abuser is not for you to stay and try to fix them! This is for you to understand that they are broken and do not want to be fixed. They love playing the victim, and we become their mothers, nurturing them like children.

Understanding that their mirroring, lies, and broken promises are manipulation tools, I need you to see the relationship for what it truly is. It's a trap! Recognising that their behaviour stems from their brokenness can help you see that the abuse is not a reflection of your worth but of the abuser's deep-seated fears and unresolved trauma.

You must reclaim your strength, recognise your value, heal, and move forward to break the cycle. Trusting your instincts and surrounding yourself with your loved ones is essential.

You deserve a relationship built on honesty, respect, and genuine love, not one based on deception and control.

I've got you $_{xx}$

My Gift

Today, dear reader, I was hoping you could write a Letter to your abuser (without sending it) expressing your feelings about the control and manipulation. This exercise can be cathartic and help you release suppressed emotions.

Physical Abuse

> "I am learning to love myself more each day. I release the past and forgive myself with compassion. My heart is open to the healing power of love. I am worthy of joy, peace, and growth. I honour my journey, and I embrace the person I am becoming. I am whole, I am enough, and I am worthy of my love."

Definition of Physical Abuse: *refers to the intentional use of physical force against another person that results in bodily injury, pain, or impairment. This type of abuse can take many forms, including hitting, slapping, punching, kicking, choking, or using objects or weapons to cause harm. It can also include actions that may not leave visible marks or injuries but cause physical discomfort or pain, such as shaking, burning, or using restraints. Physical* *abuse often occurs in the context of a power and control dynamic, where the abuser exerts dominance over the victim. It is a severe issue that can have long-term physical and psychological effects on those who experience it.*

The occurrence of intimate partner violence (IPV) is significant worldwide. According to the World Health Organization (WHO) and various studies:

Globally, about 1 in 3 women (approximately 30%) experience physical or sexual violence by an intimate partner during their lifetime.

Statistics show that millions of women worldwide are subjected to abuse by their partners each year, highlighting the widespread nature of this issue. The actual numbers may be higher, as many cases of domestic violence go unreported due to fear, shame, or other factors.

As a therapist, I often meet women who don't understand or even recognise the early signs of physical abuse. They might be in denial, thinking that a little push or nudge isn't a big deal. However, it's crucial to understand that these minor actions can lead to more severe and dangerous abuse.

My dear reader, I want to be clear: abuse is abuse. Full Stop! A push or a nudge, no matter how small it seems, is a form of physical abuse. It's a red flag that should not be ignored.

In this chapter, I share the beginning of my story, starting with the physical abuse I endured. Moving through the other chapters, you'll piece together the complete picture of my life. I'll also point out the red flags I ignored along the way, the warning signs I dismissed, and how they played a role in keeping me trapped in the cycle of abuse.

My abuse started pretty much as soon as I met him at 20 years of age. I had only left home and lived independently for about six months; I was a paralegal working in a law firm and enjoying life with my girlfriends. I must admit I was also hanging with the bad boys, but I felt safe and didn't feel intimidated, and they looked out for me. I remember one of them saying, "Go home. A girl like you shouldn't be living on her own". I thought I was fine, and I was until I met him.

I met him through a relative as she was dating his friend. Everyone seemed scared of him. He just had this darkness; he was quiet, and I was quite the social butterfly. So, he didn't seem as bad as everyone was saying. To me, he was normal (this normal was the pattern of generational abuse), but I, being Miss Naïve, didn't think anything of it and thought he was nice. He was cute, and I liked him. He was even on bail waiting to go to gaol. Yes! Score! I'm the winner! He's a badass, and he will protect me, and I will be safe with him – ***RED FLAG!***

We all hung out, and he knew I was living alone. One day, he called and said he was in trouble with the police and needed a place to stay for the night. ***RED FLAG!*** I let him stay. As I write this, I realise that if I had chosen to say no, my life might have taken a different path, much like in the movie, "Sliding Doors."

I let him in, needing to get up for work the following day. I told him he could sleep on the couch or in my bed if he preferred, as I didn't think anything of it; I was a virgin and trusted he would respect my boundaries. But he didn't. He came to bed, and before I knew it, he was on top of me. I told him to "stop", but he didn't listen. That night, I lost my virginity and not by choice. Afterwards, he didn't offer comfort or safety; he left, abandoning me. I felt lost, alone, shaken, and heartbroken, unsure of what to do or who to turn to.

After that, he acted like nothing had happened and soon moved in with me. I now realise that abusers often rush into relationships, trapping you before you have time to decide if it's what you want. ***RED FLAG!*** From that moment on, everything started to spiral downhill.

I remember his friends telling me to leave him, warning me he wasn't good for me. But how do you leave someone who's already in your home? One friend described him as "a beautiful red apple, but when you take a bite, all the worms come out." Looking back on my life from the outside, I see how painfully true that was.

While we were together, he was often abusive, pushing me around, but then he would turn around and be so considerate—making sure I was picked up from work and ensuring I was safe. But then, he would change again. ***RED FLAG!*** My life was falling apart. He was telling me my girlfriends were hitting on him and that I shouldn't trust my friends. ***RED FLAG!*** I was so confused that I didn't know what was happening or who to believe. The lies and deception were overwhelming, and it started affecting my work, but I was addicted to him. I thought I was safe with him. Crazy right? Safe!

Then, I found out he was on drugs. ***RED FLAG!*** I didn't know anything about drugs until I had to call an ambulance, and they told me he was using heroin.

I accepted it and tried to help him get off the drug. In the process, he would make me inject him and sometimes even one of his friends. ***RED FLAG!*** I had no idea what I was doing, but I was so tangled in his web that I didn't know how to leave or even go home. The shame was overwhelming. He eventually went cold turkey, and I stayed by his side, helping him through it. It was one of the most terrifying experiences of my life. That trauma bonded us in a way I never imagined.

We were evicted from my apartment, and I had to return home, feeling ashamed. My parents already knew about him, as my friends and his friends had been updating them about who I was with. Yet, they didn't do anything, which I still find strange to this day. Maybe they didn't want me back home—who knows?

When he showed up at my parents' house, asking me to leave with him, my father decided to drink with him. It almost ended in a fight. What a first impression that was! Despite everything, when I saw him again, I couldn't help but see him as my knight in shining armour. He loved me! Me! It felt incredible that someone could love me like that.

My father gave me an ultimatum: it's the family or him. Well, what would you choose? Yep, I decided my knight in shining armour would protect me, love me like no other, and we would live happily ever after. ***RED FLAG!*** My father then told me that the family was "dead to me".

Boy, was I wrong? During this time, the abuse escalated. He had me all to himself to do whatever he wanted. I lost my job, my friends, my family, and I didn't even know where we were. We had nowhere to go; he had no money, nor did I, so we ended up at his parent's house, and he kept me hidden.

We would sneak around until his father eventually caught us. He would go out, come back high, and leave me alone in his room—my entire world confined to those four walls. I felt trapped, with no money to go home if I wanted to. I was utterly alone and abandoned. Fear took over.

If he couldn't sleep, I wasn't allowed to either—he'd wake me up. If he woke up, I had to wake up, too. When he wanted to eat, we ate. I was no longer myself; I was his puppet, and he held the strings. ***RED FLAG!***

Back then, there were no mobile phones, so I couldn't even call for help. I was stuck, an empty shell, numb to everything. All I could think was, *this is it. You've chosen this, so you must make it work. He's the only one left in your life. It's just the two of us now.*

He had so much control over me that I couldn't think straight. He would compare me to his ex-girlfriend, making me feel insecure, unworthy, and not good enough. ***RED FLAG!*** Yet, we would talk about marriage and having a family, and in my deluded mind, it somehow made sense. ***RED FLAG!***

I fell pregnant almost immediately. By this point, we were back in contact with my family, so in my distorted reality, everything seemed fine. However, during my pregnancy, he became increasingly physically abusive. Even in my last trimester, he made me sleep on the floor.

No matter what I did, it was always wrong in his eyes, and he would punish me. One of his punishments was especially cruel. He would lie in bed, make me turn off the light, and then, in the dark, he'd force me to walk back to the bed, over him, and then he'd punch me. In the darkness, you can't see where the blow is coming from, so you can't move fast enough to protect yourself.

He loved to choke me. There were times I prayed he would end it—end me—so the suffering could stop. Whenever he prepared to attack, his eyes would lock onto my stomach, and all I could think was, "He's going to kill my baby".

One night, after beating me again, he forced me into an empty, freezing room. It was winter, and the cold cut through me, but fear kept me from leaving. He didn't bother locking the door; he knew I was too terrified to escape. I sat there, pregnant and shattered, sobbing in the dark, thinking, *how do I leave?* I was utterly broken.

His moods controlled my days. When he was good, it was great; when he was terrible, it was horrifying. There was no in-between, just good or bad **RED FLAG!**

He'd ignore me all day on his bad days, but the fear would set in at night. He would grind his fist or knuckle into my back or kick me until I crawled out of bed to sleep on the floor like the animal I came to be. He was careful with his abuse, avoiding my face so his parents wouldn't see the damage. I learned not to scream. Screaming only made it worse. I would suppress any sound, knowing that if I cried out, the punishment would be even more brutal.

The abuse became so routine that I could predict what kind of hell awaited me just by the way he woke up.

Nine months later, I went into labour. During those agonising hours, he was completely unsupportive. Whenever I wanted to scream from the pain, he would cover my mouth and say, "Shut up, everyone can hear you. You're embarrassing me." But there was no one else in the room. It was Boxing Day, and with minimal staff, I was left alone with this monster, abandoned yet again.

I gave birth to a beautiful baby boy. I was enveloped with love, and I felt this hope that everything would be ok that moment. After the baby was born, he ignored me: no support, no love, nothing. *I was back to reality.*

When we went home, he didn't understand the concept of having a baby; the baby needed my attention. He began getting jealous of my time with the baby, so he would have his mother take over so I could pay attention to him. It even got to the point where he wanted me to change his nappy. What?! **_RED FLAG!_** Who says that? Who is the adult, and who is the baby?

I wasn't spending any time with my baby, and I began to get mastitis; it got so bad that I ended up with a temperature, and I started shaking in bed. I was shaking so much that he kicked and pushed me out of bed. I was so sick with a temperature I stayed on the floor in the bathroom the whole night, and he didn't care.

I would wake up to feed my baby in the bathroom, sitting on the toilet in the dark, because I was too scared to wake anyone, especially him. He couldn't understand why the baby was crying, and he would blame me and how shit I was as a mother.

The final straw came when he compared me to his ex-girlfriend one too many times. Something inside me snapped. For the first time, I talked back. Suddenly, I felt an unbelievable surge of power—my fear had vanished. What was he going to do, hit me? I'd been through that hell countless times.

As I yelled, he hit me, but I kept getting back up. The more I fought back, the more furious he became until he delivered a final blow that left me dizzy and bleeding. When he saw the blood, he collapsed to the floor, crying like a child. And there I was, consoling him! ***RED BLOODY FLAG!***

Soon after, I was due for my six-week postpartum check-up. He allowed me to go but insisted on a chaperone. I was black and blue, and I still can't believe he let me leave the house like that. The doctor took one look at me, and I broke down, telling him everything. He made me call my parents, and my father's voice was clear: "Get in a cab and come home."

I took my baby in my arms, and the doctor led me out through the back of the hospital to the waiting cab. I was going home. *I am safe.*

The next couple of days are a blur. The only thing I remember clearly is the moment he showed up at my parents' house. I refused to let him in. He asked to hold the baby, and against my better judgment, I handed him over. That's when he ran. He sprinted to the car, put my baby in the front seat, and sped off. My heart stopped—my baby had been kidnapped!

I frantically called the police, and they issued a warrant, not for the kidnapping because he was the father, but for the abuse. But I was still so deluded that I didn't want to press charges or extend his gaol time. I know how that sounds now, but in that moment, my mind was still twisted by fear and confusion.

Forty-eight agonising hours later, my baby was returned to me, safe and unharmed.

Then, the love bombing started; the false hopes, the blaming of everything and everyone except him, the empty promises, the false apologies, the gifts, and the false hope of being a father and family – this was what I held onto. He told me that he couldn't live without me and threatened suicide if I didn't go back to him. I didn't want to live with that on my conscience. So, I clung to the belief that he would change.

So, I went back, and the cycle began.

Here we go again.

We found an apartment, and I moved in nine months later. Yep, it only took him nine months to convince me he had changed.

When I moved back in, the abuse started immediately. He had me under his control again, so he felt free to do whatever he wanted. But this time, I fought back. I wasn't going down without a fight. I became just as violent as he was. I was becoming him.

Soon after, I fell pregnant again. Six months later, he went to gaol, and I got to experience what giving birth was like with my mother and father by my side. What a difference.

He tried to control me from behind bars, but it didn't work. With my parents' support, I was slowly regaining my strength. This gave me the courage to stand up to him.

When he started coming out on weekends, the physical abuse began again, but this time, I fought back just as hard.

We both became violent. Finally, I reached my breaking point and refused to pick him up on the weekends. Don't get me wrong, I was still scared of the outcome when he came out of gaol, but I found the strength and left him where he belonged.

He came out of gaol six months later, and I felt sorry for him as he had nowhere to go, so I let him back in, and the cycle began again. The abuse started immediately. He was jealous of my second baby, who was then three years of age. I fell pregnant again. We finally bought our first home, but he refused to put my name on it because he wanted to punish me, so he only bought the house under his name. Go figure. I gave birth to my daughter and moved into his home, where he wanted me to pay rent.

Having my daughter saved me. I finally made the decision that I couldn't let her grow up believing that this abusive relationship was *normal*. So, I left. I went home and found a place of my own with the help of my parents. Back in the nineties, there weren't very many single mums.

I began my life. He tried for a few years to come back into my life as I was addicted to the drama and addicted to him, but at least I didn't live with him.

He became addicted to drugs again, and that's when the stalking began. He would sleep in his car, watching my every move. He ran me off the road and threw coins at my car window to smash the glass whilst driving to make me pull over. I was so terrified that I once rammed into the back of his car while trying to make it to the police station. I was living in constant fear.

I took out an AVO (Apprehended Violence Order) against him, which is just paper protection. How much does paper protect us? Let's be honest. We become so scared of *them* that we let them do whatever they want, paralysed by fear.

He was insane, worse when he was on ice (methamphetamines). One time, in front of the kids, he tore my dress right off me and dragged me down concrete stairs in a fit of rage, tearing skin off my back. My eldest son, just six years old, had to hit him in the balls to make him stop. The kids were terrified of him.

Afterwards, like clockwork, he'd break down and cry. It happened often. And somehow, I would be the one in pain, yet I would end up comforting him, feeling sorry for him. Why? Why do we suffer when they make us think we must console them?

I must add that he didn't just physically abuse people. He also abuses animals. He used to hit his first dog, and I mean punch it in the mouth; in the end, I let him run away, but I couldn't watch it. When we dated, he ran over a puppy and intentionally did it. He swerved the car and ran it over. The puppy was crying; I was saying, stop the car, and his words were, "Oh well, it shouldn't have been there" he was evil! ***BRIGHT RED FLAG!*** We bought a dog for the kids, but he would kick it and was trying to get the kids to kick it. I had to give the dog away. He is a man with no soul, pure evil.

He finally met someone else and left us alone.

A decade later, he came back. He said he missed us and wanted to be a family again. And what did I do? Yep, you guessed it—I let him back in. After ten years, I convinced myself that he must have changed. He had built a successful business and seemed to be doing well. I thought that maybe, just maybe, we could finally have the family I had always dreamed of.

But I was wrong. The cycle of abuse began all over again, dragging me back into another decade of hell. I needed to get off this roller coaster ride once and for all.

Deep down, I knew something had to change, *and that change had to be me.*

My dear reader, as you can see, it took me many years to escape the cycle of abuse. The only way I removed this addictive trauma bond and my strong value and belief in holding a family together was through hypnotherapy. This holistic modality not only helped me reclaim my life but also led me to become a hypnotherapist myself. I found my purpose, which is why I'm passionate about helping others like yourself get through this. This is also why my business partner and I created The Limitless Minds Hypno-App for women who can't get out and receive any form of therapy. With the app, women can listen to these audio programs safely in their homes. This is another powerful holistic modality that I listen to often.

My dear reader, my healing journey was challenging. We are scarred for life. Unravelling the layers is not easy, but with small steps, we get there.

Writing this chapter, I cried the whole time. Each word forced me to confront painful truths and unanswered questions:

Why did you keep going back?

What hold did he have on you?

Why didn't you leave sooner?

The frustration and anger I feel towards myself is undeniable.

Yes, I questioned my worth.

Yes, I questioned why I stayed in a cycle that broke me down.

And *yes*, I am angry that I let him darken my light for so long.

I'm sure you are even questioning me. And I understand why. My answer is simple: *I was addicted*. He was my drug. I was stuck in the delusion that he was my soulmate, that our love was real, and that sacrificing my life was proof of my love for him. I wanted so desperately to believe that we would be the perfect family. And because of that fantasy, I was willing to pay any price to make it happen.

But my dear reader, I've learned that sacrificing your life for someone who disrespects and diminishes you isn't love—*it's survival*. And it's an illusion that traps us in a cycle of pain. You are not alone in this. I see you. I know how you feel because I've been where you are.

Walking away feels like your heart is being ripped from your chest. It feels like detoxing from the drug of abuse. But here's the truth: eventually, you do *get there*. There is a miracle waiting behind every obstacle. The more significant the obstacle, the bigger the miracle.

I was lucky in many ways. My family, despite their dysfunction, stood by me and supported me through my pain. But I know not every woman has that. Some of you reading this may feel completely alone, without anyone to turn to. I want you to know that there is support out there, and there is light on the other side of this darkness.

You have the strength to step off this ride. Keep moving forward, my beautiful soul, and don't look back. No matter how hard it seems, the light waits for you to walk towards it.

If I can do it, so can you. I am with you every step of the way, guiding and supporting you.

I've got you ₓₓ

My Gift

The Heart Math Breathing Technique

The Heart Math breathing technique is designed to help you manage stress and increase emotional resilience.

Below are the steps to practice Heart Math breathing:

Find a Comfortable Position:
Sit or lie down in a comfortable position. Ensure your back is straight and your body is relaxed.

Focus on Your Heart:
Place your attention in the area of your heart. You can place your hand over your heart if that helps to deepen your focus.

Breathe Slowly and Deeply:
Begin to breathe slowly and deeply. Inhale for 5 seconds and then exhale for 5 seconds. Keep your breath smooth, steady, and even.

Activate a Positive Feeling:
While continuing to breathe, try to recall a positive memory or think about someone or something you appreciate. This could be a person, a place, or a moment that brings you joy or peace. Allow yourself to experience that positive feeling as you continue your breathing fully.

Sustain the Feeling:
Continue to breathe deeply and rhythmically to sustain this positive feeling. Focus on maintaining this state of calm and appreciation in your heart.

Practice Regularly:
Practice this breathing technique for a few minutes each day or whenever you feel stressed or anxious. The more you practice, the more naturally you can access this calm state.

This technique can help you achieve a state of unity where your heart, mind, and emotions are in sync, leading to improved mental clarity and emotional resilience.

Red Flags

"I acknowledge the red flags and trust my instincts. I choose to see clearly and honour my boundaries. I am worthy of respect and love that feels safe and true. With courage and self-love, I listen to the whispers of my intuition and act on what I know to be true."

As you read in the chapter on physical abuse, I outlined the red flags I chose to ignore in my relationship. Now, I'd like you to reflect on how many red flags you've dismissed to stay with your abuser. Or perhaps, like many of us, you chose not to see them excusing the actions and giving constant little chances. This is precisely what the abuser counts on, testing boundaries to see just how far they can push and manipulate.

Abuse isn't always evident at first. Many women find themselves deep into a toxic situation before realising what's happening. It often starts subtly, but the signs are there.

Below are some key red flags to watch for:

1. Isolation
Red Flag: Your partner isolates you from friends, family, and other support systems.

They may discourage you from seeing loved ones, criticise your friends, or make you feel guilty for spending time with others. The goal is to make you dependent on them and cut off any outside influence or perspective.

2. Control
Red Flag: Your partner tries to control aspects of your life, from your appearance to your activities.

They may dictate what you wear, who you talk to, or how you spend your time. This can include monitoring your phone, demanding passwords, or making decisions for you without your input.

3. Manipulation and Gaslighting
Red Flag: Your partner manipulates or makes you doubt your reality.

Gaslighting is when they deny things they've said or done, making you question your memory or sanity.

They may twist conversations, leaving you confused, at fault, or unsure of what's real.

4. Verbal and Emotional Abuse
Red Flag: Your partner belittles, criticises, or humiliates you regularly.

This could include name-calling, demeaning comments, or using your insecurities against you. Emotional abuse chips away at your self-esteem, making you feel unworthy of love and respect.

5. Physical Violence or Threats
Red Flag: Any form of physical aggression or threats of violence.

This includes hitting, pushing, grabbing, or any physical harm. Even if they apologise afterwards, physical abuse is never acceptable. Threats of violence, even if not acted upon, are also abusive.

6. Sexual Coercion or Abuse
Red Flag: Your partner pressures or forces you into sexual activities you're uncomfortable with.

This includes anything from pressuring you for sex, making you feel guilty for saying no, to outright assault. Consent is vital, and any violation of your sexual boundaries is a serious red flag.

7. Extreme Jealousy and Possessiveness

Red Flag: Your partner exhibits excessive jealousy or possessiveness.

They may accuse you of cheating without reason, demand to always know your whereabouts, or become irrationally angry when you interact with others. This behaviour is rooted in insecurity and is another form of control.

8. Blame-Shifting

Red Flag: Your partner never takes responsibility for their actions and blames you for their behaviour.

They might say, "You made me do this," or "If you hadn't done that, I wouldn't have reacted this way." This tactic justifies their abuse and shifts the responsibility onto you.

9. Rapid Escalation of the Relationship

Red Flag: The relationship moves very quickly, with intense declarations of love early on.

It may seem romantic at first, but this could be a tactic to make you feel deeply committed before you know the person. They might pressure you to move in together, get engaged, or make significant commitments too soon.

10. Threats of Self-Harm or Suicide

Red Flag: Your partner threatens to harm themselves if you leave or don't comply with their demands.

Statements like "I'll kill myself if you leave" or "I can't live without you" are manipulative. These threats trap you in the relationship by exploiting your empathy and concern.

These red flags are often dismissed or *explained away* because we want to believe in the potential for change. However, recognising these behaviours for what they are can be the first step toward breaking free. It's not about blaming yourself for not seeing them sooner; it's about becoming aware of the red flags.

I've got you $_{xx}$

My Gift

Today, dear reader, I encourage you to take a moment to write down and list both your abuser's good and bad qualities. As you compare the two, you'll see which side outweighs the other. This exercise can help you recognise the red flags you've been overlooking.

Sexual Abuse

"I honour my body, mind, and soul. I deserve respect, safety, and love. I release any pain and reclaim my power. I am whole, I am strong, I am free."

Definition of Sexual Abuse: *Sexual abuse is any form of non-consensual sexual contact or behaviour, including physical acts like touching, fondling, rape, or attempted rape. It also encompasses actions that exploit, humiliate, or harm a person sexually, such as forced exposure to pornography, sexual harassment, or inappropriate sexual comments. Sexual abuse can occur between strangers or within relationships, including marriages and families. It's important to note that sexual abuse is a violation of a person's autonomy, dignity, and rights, and it often leaves deep emotional and psychological scars.*

My dear reader, I want you to know that what you're experiencing is not okay. Sexual abuse, no matter how it happens or who it comes from, is a violation of your body, your trust, and your soul. It is not something you deserve or something you must put up with. I understand you are doing this to keep the peace. I get it; I did it. You are not to blame for the actions of someone who chooses to harm you.

Your body is yours alone, and no one has the right to take that away from you!!

During my time growing up, I had many occasions where I had been sexually abused. I recall a time when I was on the train going to school, and the train was so full that I had this Asian man rubbing himself on me. I felt so violated, and I didn't speak up! I just allowed it to happen.

Why?

Another occasion was when I went to the Easter Show with my brother, a neighbour, and his friend. They were much older. After the show, his friend sat in the back with me, and my brother sat in the front. While he was in the back, he groomed me, telling me it was okay while rubbing and moving his hand up my leg until I flinched. I felt sick and once again didn't say anything!

Why?

I question myself: why? Back then, if we had mentioned anything of the kind, we were *making it up*, or no one would listen. Plus, I was a people-pleaser and didn't want to disappoint anyone or cause problems, so I allowed it to happen.

As you already know, my dear reader, how I lost my virginity, I once again allowed this monster to violate me and take away the precious moments that you are supposed to give to someone you love. This memory will stay with me forever. ***NO MEANS NO!***

His excuse was that I *shouldn't have flirted* with him, and *everyone was calling me a slut* because most of my friends were guys. Let's make it clear here, just because I had a lot of male friends didn't mean I was a 'slut'.

Growing up, I was a tomboy and enjoyed hanging with the guys. So, the correct answer to his idiotic reasoning was, "I shouldn't have let you into my apartment to help you"! Once again, those "sliding doors" appear. I always think, what if? What if I didn't let him in? What would my life be? How would my life have turned out?

Well, my dear reader, we will never know, but I do know that my life purpose was to experience what I did so that I could write this book for you. And I can be your voice to tell you that *it's okay, it gets better*, you are not alone, and *this too shall pass*.

As you read in the physical abuse chapter, I was deeply trauma-bonded from that point onward. The manipulation, the breadcrumbs, the gaslighting—I was utterly hooked. The more trauma I endured, the more entwined I was in the web. Being naïve and vulnerable combined with a manipulative man, we tend only to see their truth, not what we believe in our hearts. Our intuition screams at us, but we ignore it.

Once again, I allowed myself to be sexually abused as I didn't want to cause problems, and he convinced me that this was normal. After that, it hurt all the time, and there was no intimacy at all. He just abused me like an object, and I thought this was normal. I couldn't understand what women loved about it. And now he had moved in, so I was stuck with this abusive man that has taken my virginity, my dignity, and my self-worth had depleted. He didn't work, so I looked after us, paying for everything.

He had me hook, line, and sinker.

The objectification continued until I finally left him after my first child was born. But during the abuse, every time I tried to leave or even get out of the room, he would block the door and force me into making a deal. That deal always involved the sexual acts he wanted to perform, and I would agree just to be set free. So he would violate me violently whilst I sobbed, but he didn't care. He kept going, and in the end, he would refuse to let me go. Looking back, I realise this was self-sabotage, trying to survive an unbearable situation. Alongside the physical abuse, I was subjected to every other form of abuse as well.

I'm sharing this with you, dear reader, because I want to be honest, raw and vulnerable to you and share my story so you can understand that any form of abuse is never acceptable.

Don't get me wrong; he would lure me back whenever I left, and the love bombing began. Remember again the Fox and the Rabbit'. This was my relationship. The intimacy felt incredible. The gifts, the holidays, the "*I love you's*", the apologies, and the promises to change all pulled me back into the cycle. I'm sure you've heard it all before: "I didn't mean it," "Forgive me," "It won't happen again." But once you go back, everything changes. I became an object once more, lying there till it was over. The less I wanted it, the more he did it. It was a twisted game.

I remember once, during one of his love-bombing phases, he would take me on these amazing holidays, flying first class to New York. One time, he said to me, "Well, you're cheaper than a prostitute!" and that was supposed to be a compliment. I wondered if that was his twisted way of showing love. My denial kicked in, telling me, "Come on, he didn't mean it like that. Of course, he loves you. That's why he abuses you all the time. This is normal, right?" In front of everyone, the facade was that of the "husband of the century," people would say, "Oh, you're so lucky; he spoils you." While I am incredibly grateful for having the experience of flying first class and experiencing these holidays, the reality is that it was all a mask to cover the truth.

To me, he was like a predator in the night on heat. Any slight move I made would set him off, and he would want it anywhere and everywhere. The more I said no, the more it turned him on. He loved the chase. It made me sick. I could share so many more stories, but unfortunately, my dear reader, I think I've said enough for you to understand how these predators groom you from the start, making you feel like this twisted reality is normal.

As a therapist, I hear my clients speak about being used as objects, too, sometimes through being coerced into getting high or bringing in other partners without their consent. I understand that feeling all too well. I needed copious amounts of alcohol just to become intimate with him because, without it, I was nothing more than a body, a soulless vessel for him to satisfy his desires.

I know this is confronting, but I need to speak about it because we are human beings with feelings and a soul.

True intimacy is far more than just a physical act. It's the deep connection of trust, respect, and love.

When two people come together in genuine intimacy, there is a beautiful energy exchange. Two souls join as one, feeling seen, valued, and appreciated. It's about vulnerability, safety, and mutual care; the experience is euphoric.

Being sexually abused by your partner is the opposite of intimacy. It's not about connection or love. It's about bloody control, power, and degradation. It shatters your soul, leaving you feeling violated and stripped of your self-worth. Instead of feeling connected, you feel numb, empty, and lost. What should be a moment of shared tenderness becomes a source of deep pain and confusion, making you question your worth.

True intimacy builds you up, makes you feel alive and want to live, a feeling of freedom while abuse tears you down. It's crucial to understand this difference because no one deserves to have their soul destroyed under the pretence of what should be a loving connection.

To this day, I still do not know nor have I ever made love, but my body and soul long for it. I am sure having a partner who truly loves and connects with you on all levels would feel exhilarating.

My Gift

Today, dear reader, I was hoping you could write a letter to yourself and be your best friend. What would you write? What would you tell yourself? What would your silver linings look like? This exercise helps you practice self-compassion, gain clarity, validate your emotions, and find strength in your journey toward healing and empowerment.

You've got this xx

Remember Your Worth

Walking away isn't a sign of weakness; it reflects your inner strength. You don't leave to prove your value to others. You go because you've finally recognised your worth.

Never hesitate to stand alone if needed. The actual pain isn't in losing someone you care for; it's in losing yourself by valuing them too much and forgetting how special you are.

Honour your worth, stand in your power, and always be true to who you are. Be clear about what you want, and never settle for anything less than what you deserve.

Your time, energy, and love are precious. Invest them in relationships with people who genuinely respect and uplift you. You don't need a crowd to be happy, just a few who truly appreciate the real you!

When you fully realise your worth, everything in your life changes. Don't accept mediocrity. Take bold steps, follow your passion, and let it lead you to a life that fulfils you!

Yes, *You!*

You weren't meant to merely exist, so set your path ablaze with purpose and never look back.

I've got you ₓₓ

Emotional and Psychological Abuse

"Each day, I reclaim my strength and worth, embracing the love and respect I deserve. I am healing, growing, and empowered, and my past does not define my future."

Definition of emotional abuse: *Emotional abuse in an abusive relationship encompasses behaviours that severely undermine a person's self-worth, mental health, and autonomy. It includes verbal attacks such as insults and constant criticism aimed at degrading the victim's self-esteem, as well as manipulation tactics that use guilt, shame, or fear to control their actions. Emotional abuse often involves isolating the victim from friends and family to increase their dependence on the abuser and gaslighting, which makes the victim doubt their perceptions and* *reality. Additionally, threats and intimidation are used to maintain control, while emotional neglect involves withholding affection and validation to make the victim feel unworthy. These actions can be as damaging as physical abuse, eroding the victim's confidence and sense of safety.*

"If you are giving your all to someone who doesn't recognise it, you are giving it to the wrong person".

My analogy for emotional and psychological abuse is like a child with a doll. When the child wants to show the doll off, she dresses it in pretty clothes, ensuring it looks perfect. But when they're back home, and the doll is no longer needed, it gets put away in a cupboard. Sometimes, the child shakes the doll out of frustration—maybe because the doll didn't "behave" the way the child wanted, or maybe because the child was just in a bad mood.

But when it's time to show the doll off again, the child takes it out, brushes its hair, and dresses it up, making sure it looks good for everyone to see. The doll has to look perfect, even if it's been shaken and ignored when no one else is around.

This is how emotional and psychological abuse can feel. You're only valued when it suits the abuser, and once you're no longer needed, you're pushed aside. But when it's time to "perform" again, you're expected to look perfect, hiding all the hurt underneath, just like that doll.

Emotional abuse is exhausting, both mentally and physically. It depletes your self-worth and can make you feel like you're going crazy. And yes, my dear reader, we do go bloody crazy!! Our mental state is so worn down from all the gaslighting and the breadcrumbs offered to us.

What are Gaslighting and Breadcrumbing?

Gaslighting and breadcrumbing are two different tactics that the abuser uses in the relationship.

Gaslighting is when the abuser manipulates you into doubting yourself. They make you question your memories, feelings, or perceptions, often to gain control over you. The goal is to make you feel confused and dependent on them. Can you relate? This is such a common tactic they use in their little game.

An example of gaslighting is when you clearly remember conversing with them about a party you were invited to. However, when you get ready for the party, they ask, "Where are you going?" and you reply, "I told you, and you said I could go". They insist that we never told them that we *must imagine things and are losing our minds*. We begin to question ourselves, for example, "Did I tell him? I am sure I did. I'm sure he said it was ok". So now we don't trust our thoughts, and the abuser must be right, so in the end, we don't go to the party because he didn't know about it and never said we could go in the first place.

Breadcrumbs, on the other hand, are when the abuser gives you just enough attention, affection or promises to keep you but never follows through. They make you think there's hope for a better relationship, but it never develops. The goal is to keep you around without making real commitments because they cannot commit to anything.

An example of a breadcrumb is when the abuser might occasionally send you sweet messages, send you flowers or promise to take you to a party with them so you can meet their friends. However, they never follow through with their promise, so you are waiting for the time when they do. This leaves you feeling like you aren't good enough to meet their friends. Still, it's not that at all; they can't commit to you, so why do you need to meet their friends? You're left waiting for those moments, hoping things will get better, but they keep giving you just enough to make you stay without fully committing.

As a therapist, I often listen to women who have been deeply affected by emotional and psychological abuse. Their stories are filled with so much pain, confusion, and a profound loss of self-worth. Listening to them, I completely understand how this kind of abuse can break us down from the inside.

Through my Trauma Healing Program, which includes HypnoQi, I've helped women release their trauma and rebuild their self-worth. With each session, they began to see themselves not as victims but as the resilient, powerful women they are. I am so bloody proud of every one of them!

I recall my abuser's last words to me before we finally ended the relationship, that he didn't realise that he still had to keep working on the relationship once he got me back. He thought he only had to try hard to get me back. Then, once he had me back, he didn't have to try anymore. Do you believe him? Nope, I don't. Any excuse will do.

They excuse all their actions and never take accountability. My abuser knew that no matter how badly he treated me, I would always take him back. He thought, *"If I treat her like shit, she'll leave for a while, but I'll just chase after her, and she'll come back."* And sadly, he was right—I always went back, and he knew it.

Remember the fox and the rabbit? It's the thrill of the chase he was addicted to, and when you look at it from the outside in, I guess I loved how he chased because I was addicted to the love bombing and how he used to make me feel. The validation, the love, the affection, the intimacy. He would become the perfect man, and it would all change once he had me back. That emotional roller coaster becomes exhausting.

I wasn't the only one on this ride; unfortunately, my children were also on this emotional roller coaster. There were the empty promises and the no-shows for birthdays and graduations.

One of my children missed his Schoolies trip to Fiji because he refused to sign his passport. For those unfamiliar, Schoolies is a big tradition in Australia where students celebrate finishing Year 12 with a week-long trip or party, often at popular destinations like Fiji. Why would you put your children through something like this? Who does this? Why punish your children? I will never understand.

The other received his law degree and was passing the bar—a massive milestone in his legal career—but his father missed it for a petty excuse, which was so bloody trivial it was unbelievable. He didn't even try to change his plans. I ask, who does that? A man who doesn't know how to be a father that's who.

The milestones he was invited to, yet missed, leaving my children feeling abandoned and rejected, broke my heart. Why did he come back? To show what? To prove what—that he's wealthy? So what? Look at what he's missing: the true riches, his children, with whom he now has no relationship. This will be the story he tells his next victim—that his children and partner have cut ties, painting us as the villains. But the real question is, will she ask why? Will she question how things got to this point? Or will she listen and feel sorry for him? What do you think she'll do?

Remember, the abuser chooses someone just like us. What did we do? We believed every word, never questioning their distorted stories. We trust ourselves, so we extend that trust to our abuser.

He made it incredibly difficult for me to maintain a relationship with my middle son because he was so envious of him. I couldn't understand why. I treated all my kids equally, but he couldn't see it. He constantly put our son down, and despite all his efforts to earn his father's love and validation, unfortunately, his father never saw him for who he was.

Once, I wanted to surprise him, so I left early, drove into the city, an hour away from my home, and cleaned his house from top to bottom. I left him a gift on the bench and then returned home to the kids. All I received was a text that said, 'Thanks. ' There was no phone call, no 'thank you,' no 'I love you'—nothing.

Another time, I was out Christmas shopping with the kids and started to panic because I was running late. My anxiety was through the roof. I had told him when I'd be home, and when I called, he was already in a bad mood. I knew he would punish me with the silent treatment when I returned.

He loved using the silent treatment, ignoring me and the kids for days. I would ask him what was wrong if he wanted to talk, and he would reply, "I am talking." When I pointed out that he hadn't spoken to me, he would say, "I'm speaking now, I answer you—isn't that enough?" It drove me crazy.

Back then, I had to write him letters because if I spoke, he would twist my words until I felt completely overwhelmed and lost in what I was trying to say. His constant gaslighting left me confused and defeated, making it feel like speaking up wasn't worthwhile.

He played with my mind so much that I was going crazy. Trying to run the household, protecting my children from him, and dealing with his immaturity and his behaviours were exhausting; along with the gaslighting, I began to stutter; I was losing my mind, and he would tell the kids, "It's ok, mummy is just sick, we must look after her". The kids would be so scared because they thought *we would have to be with him if I lost Mummy*. They would tell me, "Mummy, please don't be sick", and they would try to help me, but the only person who could help me was myself. I needed to leave before it was too late. Sometimes, I couldn't even get out of bed, which was hard.

I remember Mother's Day; the kids were very young. They were trying to make breakfast for me to bring to bed, and I told him to go downstairs and help them before they hurt themselves. He said, "What for? You're not my mother." So I went downstairs to help them and bring it to me in bed. He never acknowledged every other Mother's Day up to today because I wasn't his mother.

Valentine's Day was non-existent, and I craved so much just to be acknowledged on this day. I just wanted one day to be loved and seen, but no, he would not speak to me on this day, giving me the silent treatment to really make sure he broke my heart. These were the days when I thought he didn't love me. He hated me or loved punishing me.

There were times when he played cruel mind games with me, telling me he had children with other women. Once, he told me that he had a child with his ex-girlfriend, the one he consistently compared me to, while he was in gaol, and I had just had my second child. It devastated me, and I didn't know whether it was true, but it was a lie. Then, after I came back a decade later, he told me again that he had another child with another woman and that this child didn't even know he was the father.

It's hard to believe these lies, but the emotional and psychological torment messes with your mind.

With the constant rejection and neglect you feel being in the relationship, you lose your identity as not only yourself but as a human being. You become so numb to the world that it feels like Groundhog Day every day; you are just there, existing in this world, not knowing where you went wrong, questioning yourself, how did I get here? What am I going to do? The thoughts of suicide consistently entered my mind, and the only thing holding me back from this was my children, and the idea of leaving them with this monster was out of the question. So, I just had to keep going for them.

I was in a relationship with a man and had never felt so alone and unsupported. When I expressed my feelings, he would respond, "Oh well, that's your problem, not mine. It's you; fix yourself." I thought that if I became more affectionate, things might improve, but that would only last for a little while. The only time he wanted to be loving was during intimate moments. I often found myself watching other couples, envying the simple gestures like a man kissing his partner on the forehead. Those small acts of affection were reminders of what had been taken away from me—respect, love, and everything else that matters. Abusers take your soul!

So many times, he would say, "Come over, and I'll take you out for dinner." I would get ready and rush to his place, only to walk in and find him in his pyjamas. When asked, "What are you doing?" he would reply casually, "What?" I'd respond, "I thought we were going out for dinner." And he would say, "I changed my mind."

Another time, we were heading out, and since he lived in the city, he preferred to walk everywhere. He insisted I wear heels to look nice, so I would bring my flat shoes to change into until we reached the restaurant. On this particular day, as we walked, he suddenly looked at me and said, "You look like you're going to the beach." I was shocked and replied, "I have my heels in my hands!" He said, "I'm not walking with you looking like this," and walked off.

When I couldn't find him, I thought he was joking and assumed he would be waiting at the restaurant. I put on my heels and headed there, but he wasn't there when I arrived. I called him—no answer. I messaged him—no reply. Frustrated, I organised a cab and went back home. I couldn't deal with him anymore. Thank God I wasn't living with him at the time.

After a decade apart, I remember when he returned, claiming he missed and loved the family. His first words were, "Gee, you've put on weight," although I was still quite slim. He then bragged about being with women much skinnier than me and admitted he was using me to get closer to the kids. I was stunned. Despite this, I gave this man another fifteen years of my life.

There were countless times when I had to defend myself to my loved ones because of the lies and stories he fabricated about me. He was a master manipulator, and I constantly justified my actions to others. I ended up looking like the crazy, psycho wife while he played the innocent victim, dealing with my supposed "moods." Do you feel me on this one, dear reader? I know you've been through this, too.

When COVID hit, he acted like I had some contagious disease, so I had to stay home. I was so sick, and I had to beg him to do some grocery shopping for me because I could barely function. He never asked how I was, never checked if I needed anything. He just looked at me like I was contaminated.

He brought the groceries once, so let's give him a round of applause. But instead of leaving them at my front door, he left them in my garage, forcing me to walk down the stairs, aching and struggling, to bring them up myself. It was excruciating, but I had no choice—I couldn't leave the house, but he made it more complicated than it needed to be.

I remember a couple of times when we talked about moving in. I'd get myself mentally prepared, even seeing a psychologist because I was scared. I knew I needed to be vulnerable with him, even though I didn't fully trust him. But I wanted to move in to make my life easier, and I did love him very much—though it was a distorted kind of love.

So often, I would just be about to move in with him, and he would change his mind and gaslight me with his famous words, "We never discussed this".

The first time I travelled overseas, I was flying to New York to meet him. He would go there every year, and I was finally joining him this time. We fought a month before the trip, and he became distant, leaving me unsure whether I should even get on the plane. My anxiety was through the roof; I was terrified that once I arrived, he wouldn't be there. He was already in New York and was uncontactable—no calls, no messages—so I went on the plane, not knowing what to expect. I even had a backup plan in case he decided not to show up, but thankfully, he did.

The trip itself was great, allowing me to forget everything that had happened. However, when we returned, he ignored me for three months. This was yet another ritual in our relationship. It felt like I never got a chance to enjoy anything, even our holidays.

I don't know about you, my dear reader, but for me, my abuser always turned to a priest whenever I left him, seeking help to get us back together. He would attend church every Sunday as if that could make everything right for him. He promised to see psychologists and doctors, and we even attended marriage counselling once. However, during that session, he completely ridiculed me in front of the counsellor, and we never went back.

He put on a show, pretending to seek help and improve, but everything changed as soon as I returned. He would stop seeing the priest, quit going to church, ignore the psychologist he claimed to be visiting, and stop taking his medication. It was all just a facade to lure me back in, after which he would revert to being the person he always was.

Breaking my spirit and watching my kids suffer made me question what I was doing. I felt utterly stuck—so much so that I couldn't find a way off this tormenting ride by the end. My children became the turning point in the most significant decision I had to make. When they decided not to speak to me, it was the most important wake-up call I could have received. Losing my kids, my team, my best friends—my heart—was not something I could accept. I realised I had to jump off the ride; my children saved me from the relentless spiral of mental torment. I was going crazy, and I feared for myself.

There are countless stories I could share about the emotional abuse I endured, but I would need to write an entire book just on that. My dear reader, the lesson here is simple: they do not change! Enough is enough—no more!

We often feel sorry for them and excuse their actions because they were raised in dysfunctional families. But so were we! Yet, we didn't play the victim; we soldiered on like warriors. So why do we tolerate emotional abuse?

As a therapist, looking from the outside in, I now see that the abuser cannot love you properly because, deep down, they are intimidated by your potential. They feel threatened by the strength and brilliance they see in you. Instead of lifting you, they compete with you, knowing that if they genuinely support you, you would realise your worth, and they would lose their hold on you.

They enter your life during a moment of vulnerability, pretending to be exactly what you need. But the truth is, they will drain your energy and hold you back because without you, their world crumbles. You find yourself sleeping next to someone who sees your power and fears it—someone who knows that if you rise to your full potential, you will be far too much of a woman for them to handle.

That's why they never celebrate your victories, clap for you, or encourage or support you. They know you would outgrow your strength if you fully embraced them. You don't need them to shine; you never did. It's time to recognise that power within you and let go of anyone who doesn't want to see you soar.

You are not alone; I am with you. Let's soar through life together.

I've got you $_{xx}$

My Gift

Today, dear reader, after reading about emotional and psychological abuse, I would suggest a self-reflection exercise where you identify the specific ways you have experienced manipulation, gaslighting, or control.

I encourage you to:

1. *Journal your emotions, reflecting on how these experiences have impacted your self-esteem, trust, and mental well-being.*

2. *Identify Patterns and write down recurring behaviours that may have been dismissed but are now recognised as abusive.*

3. *Create a list of emotional boundaries you wish to establish in relationships, focusing on what behaviours you will no longer tolerate.*

This exercise helps you process the abuse and empowers you to set healthier boundaries.

Verbal Abuse

"If you stand for a reason, be prepared to stand alone like a tree, and if you fall on the ground, fall like a seed that grows back to fight again!"

Definition of verbal abuse: *Verbal abuse is a form of emotional and psychological harm where one person uses words to control, demean, manipulate, or hurt another person. This can include insults, threats, belittling comments, constant criticism, yelling, name-calling, or any other language to undermine the other person's self-esteem or mental well-being. Verbal abuse can be subtle or overt, and it often erodes the victim's confidence and sense of self over time.*

The Nursery Rhyme:
'Stick and Stones may break my bones, but words will never hurt me'.

"Sticks and stones may break my bones, but words will never hurt me." This familiar nursery rhyme, which has been around for generations, was meant to teach children resilience. The message was clear: physical pain might hurt, but the words of others should not affect us. However, the reality of verbal abuse tells a different story.

As a therapist, I see how words have so much power. It has the power to uplift you and the power to destroy you. When words are used as weapons, and dear reader, our abuser loves using their words, they can cause deep, invisible wounds that hold onto us long after the physical bruises have healed. I would sometimes say to myself I would prefer to be hit than deal with the verbal, emotional and psychological abuse. Verbal abuse is often dismissed because it doesn't leave visible marks, but its impact can be just as, if not more, damaging than physical abuse.

Verbal abuse is more than just harsh words; it is their way of diminishing our self-worth, manipulating our emotions, and using control. The constant bombardment of criticism, insults, and threats slowly wears us down, making us feel stuck and abandoned.

The fundamental trauma manifests in anxiety, depression, and a profound loss of identity. We completely lose ourselves in the relationship; they create the other version of us, and we consistently think about the hurtful words in our minds, internalising the abuse until we believe it is true.

When verbal, emotional, and psychological abuse are combined, the impact can be overwhelming. The abuser uses words not just to insult or belittle us but to undermine our entire sense of reality and self-worth. Over time, we become trapped in the cycle of self-doubt, fear, and confusion, feeling like we are losing ourselves piece by piece.

Emotionally, we become depleted because we are denied the validation or affection that could help us regain our sense of self. The abuser often creates an emotional rollercoaster, offering occasional kindness or apologies only to withdraw them again, leaving us constantly searching for the next moment of relief; this is where I believe the addiction begins. This, my dear reader, is the power of manipulation that creates the trauma bond, where we now feel we cannot leave despite how painful it is.

The rhyme "sticks and stones" may have intended to build emotional resilience, but it fails to recognise that words can hurt deeply. The emotional and psychological scars left by verbal abuse can take time to heal, primarily through HypnoQi. By releasing all those scars, negative thoughts, stuck emotions and especially those limiting beliefs, they have instilled in us. Imagine that: no more triggers, no more scars, finding your identity, understanding who you are, learning to love yourself again, peace and just healing.

For example, imagine someone constantly being told, "You're worthless," or "No one else will ever love you." These words may seem cruel on the surface, but their psychological impact is overwhelming. When accompanied by gaslighting, where the abuser denies, twists, or manipulates reality, we begin to question our perceptions. We start to believe that maybe we are the problem or unlovable.

When I finally decided to leave him, the words he spoke to me were meant to break me. He said, "No one will love you like I do. The men out there will use you and leave you. They don't want to bring up someone else's kids. They'll judge you for being a single mum. Who's going to love someone with kids? You have nothing to offer." Now, remember when I left him the first time? There were no single mothers back in my day, so I believed him.

Recently, He tried to convince me that we had been through too much together to move on. "We're too old to start over," he insisted. "I'm the only one who will look after you how you deserve. I will be the one to look after you when you are old. No one will treat you like I have. Who's going to want you when you have nothing materially to offer? You're too crazy. Only I can deal with you." I thank God now, as I look from the outside in, if he can't look after me correctly while I am healthy, what on earth would he do to me whilst being old and incapable of looking after myself?

He attacked every part of me. "You're too fat to go to a wedding—do we need to use the curtains to make your clothes? Look at you, always making something out of nothing. What did you do now? Why did you tell them what I've done? No one will believe you. You're the crazy one. You're the one with issues. You're the one who can't love properly, who can't hold down a relationship."

When he compared me to others, he twisted the knife even deeper into my soul, making me believe I was not good enough. "I'm keeping in touch with her because she's so much better than you. She has a degree. What do you have? Nothing. You're a shit mother. Your cooking is shit. You can't even clean properly. Why did you buy me that? You obviously don't know me that well."

Every word was designed to make me feel small, worthless, and incapable. "You're always bringing up the past. You can't get over it. You're just like your mother, exactly like your father. Your family is shit. Your friends are shit. They keep looking at me because they want me. When we move in together, there'll be no going out with your friends."

Even in the most minor details, he found a way to criticise. "Why did you clean this that way? F*ck, you can't do anything right. Why did you step on the rug like that? Look at your dirty feet. Why are you walking like that? You've dirtied it now. Where have you been in those clothes? You can't sit on the lounge with those clothes."

Oh, the best part was I couldn't sing in the car or dance; "What are you doing? You look like an idiot. Don't sing! Even if I hummed, he would say "sing internally, no humming". So, guess what I do now? I bloody sing at the top of my lungs and dance to great tunes in my car! Freedom is priceless!

He belittled my role as a mother and my entire existence. "You think being a single mum is something special? You're just a mum; it's not hard. What have you done all day? I work, and you sit on your arse looking after kids. Why is he crying? See, you can't even be a good mum."

I would be in the kitchen, and he would be over me, watching me like a hawk: *You're cutting the carrots wrong, doing this wrong, that wrong.* Gosh, I couldn't breathe without him telling me how to breathe.

Nothing I did was ever good enough. He even controlled my time. "You need to be here now, or I'm leaving without you." I'd finish work at four and rush to meet him in the city by five, barely having time to change. And then, he'd say, "You never wear your hair down. You look tired. Can't you wear something different? You always wear the same thing." I remember walking in with Ugg boots, and he scolded me for looking like a junkie.

His nagging, endless complaints, and relentless judgment were exhausting. Living with him felt like being trapped in a never-ending storm of negativity. But now, being away from him, I realise how draining he was. I've never had so much energy, and my mind has never been clearer. It's like a weight has been lifted off my shoulders, and I can finally breathe again.

His compulsion for negativity disgusts me now. It's as if he thrived on tearing everything down, never once letting a positive word slip from his mouth. The irony is almost laughable: men like him complain about women being nagging, but in truth, they are far worse or at least he was.

They project their misery onto us, blaming us for the very negativity they create. Now that I'm free from his toxic influence, I see it all so clearly, and I'm thankful every day for the peace I've reclaimed.

My dear reader, every word and insult is a projection of his insecurities, fears, and self-hatred. He wanted me to feel as low as he did inside. But as I look back, I see those words didn't reflect me. They reflect him.

Nothing I did was ever good enough for him. But that was because nothing would ever be good enough to fill the void inside him.

Dear reader, you must understand that when anyone, not just the abuser, is verbally abusing you, I want you to notice the words they use and how it often reflects how they see themselves, not how they see you. Abusers tend to project their negative feelings and perceptions onto others. This means they might accuse you of things they're doing or struggling with internally.

My Gift

Today, I encourage you to really listen the next time your abuser speaks, especially when they begin to criticise or hurt you. What are they genuinely saying? What do their words reveal about their inner struggles and fears? Please, don't accept the painful things they say as your truth. Understand, dear reader, that their words often reflect more about them than about you. This is their pain speaking, not a reflection of your worth.

Understanding this can change how you view the abuse. You'll start to see that their words aren't a reflection of who you are but a reflection of who they are and how they feel about themselves. This knowledge can help you protect yourself emotionally and begin the process of healing. When you hear their words for what they are—projections of their own insecurities—you can start to take back your power and move forward with your life. So, let's take your power back together!!!

I've got you xx

Financial Abuse

> "I am worthy of financial freedom and respect. I am reclaiming my power and taking steps toward independence. I deserve to make my own financial decisions and build a secure future. My strength and resilience guide me towards a life of financial empowerment and self-worth."

Definition of Financial Abuse in an abusive relationship:
Financial abuse in an abusive relationship refers to the use of financial control and manipulation to exert power and maintain dominance over a partner. This can include restricting access to money or financial resources, controlling spending and financial decisions, sabotaging employment or job opportunities, accumulating debt in the partner's name, and isolating them from financial

support systems. Financial abuse undermines the victim's economic independence and security, reinforcing the power imbalance in the relationship and making it more difficult for them to leave or assert control over their own life.

The financial abuse began almost immediately after I met him. I was a paralegal earning a decent income, and I had never known real financial struggles, having come from a comfortable family. But when he moved in, it wasn't long before I found myself paying for everything—rent, groceries, bills. It was as though the responsibility of our entire life together fell squarely on my shoulders.

One day, after he had taken more of my money, I asked him for just $10 for coffee. His reaction was explosive, and he completely lost it. That moment demonstrated to me the turning point of my life. I began to withdraw from social activities and stop going out because every cent I earned was being focused on his demands, dinners, our rent, and everything we needed to maintain our lives together.

Eventually, I left my job and started a new position at another law firm in the city, but that didn't last long. His criminal activities were catching up to us, and soon, the police were involved. My parents even called them, hoping to scare me into coming home. But by then, I was trapped in his web.

He 'apparently' couldn't work due to his bail conditions and supposed mental state going to gaol; well, that's what his excuse was. So, I was the sole breadwinner. I was the one who paid for everything, including our wedding bands. No, I never received a diamond engagement ring like ordinary people. I never even married correctly. We just ended up at a registry. I had no friends or family there, and oh man, was he in a bad mood that day.

My so-called celebration of marriage was absolute shit! Now, is that a massive red flag, dear reader? Yes, it bloody is, but no, *Nicole needed to stay cause maybe he might change after we are married.* What a fool I was.

The way he proposed wasn't romantic; it was desperate. "Hey, you want to get married so we can get the police off our backs?" he asked. When I realised this was his proposal idea, I still said yes. I thought this was it—he was the one for me. My parents had distanced themselves, and I had no friends left, so I clung to him as my only lifeline.

After we married and our baby was born, he decided we should start a cleaning business. But, as with everything else, the work fell to me. I went from being a paralegal to scrubbing floors on my hands and knees and cleaning houses while he did nothing. I remember one day cleaning a home for a very particular woman. I was on the floor, scrubbing like Cinderella, when he came in and told me to get up—we were leaving. That was the end of the cleaning business.

When he went to gaol, he left me in a $20,000.00 debt. He bought all this expensive furniture because, in his head, as he used to say, "Why should I do without?" So I paid again, struggling on the single-parent pension, trying to pay off a debt, rent, and, at the time, caring for my two boys.

He was on work release, and I thought, *great, he can start giving me some money so I can survive* - but no, he was saving it for himself because he didn't know if he wanted to be with me anymore and needed the money. Go figure. I would pick him up like the good wife I was every weekend with a toddler and a baby. He would come out with enough money to buy us food for the weekend, and you know what he did? Yep, he would make sure everything was finished before he went back in.

He was finally released from gaol, and of course, we were together, but he had spent all the money on court fees as they were going to extend his sentence due to his physical abuse of me whilst being released on weekends.

He decided to buy a truck and start his own business. He began making money, but it was all for him. I was still on a pension, paying rent and supporting the kids. Meanwhile, he saved his money and bought his first home, even though we were still married. His exact words were, "I found a loophole to f*ck women up."

Did I run? No. By now, you're probably thinking, "She just doesn't learn." And you'd be right. I had no boundaries left and had stopped caring about everything, including myself. I was numb to the world, living in constant denial, and addicted to the hope that things would somehow change.

After I gave birth to my daughter, we moved into 'his' house. But anytime I did something he didn't like, his go-to line was, "This is my house. If you don't like it, leave" (well, not exactly in those words, but I am sure you know what I mean) or "There's the door." So, I left him again. Having my daughter made me realise I couldn't let her grow up thinking that this kind of relationship was typical or that it was acceptable for a man to treat a woman the way he treated me. After that, we never lived together again.

During his drug-induced days, he was out partying, spending money on drugs instead of providing for us. He didn't give me money for the kids but somehow had enough for his habits. Behind my back, he would take money from the kids, threatening them to stay quiet. My eldest son was especially worried about the money he'd saved from tooth fairy gifts and Christmas because his father had a pattern of taking it and never giving it back.

It wasn't until my son found the courage to tell me what was happening that I confronted him. He exploded in rage, becoming extremely abusive toward both my son and me.

Now, dear reader, ask yourself why he would react like that. He was guilty and didn't know how to handle it like an adult, so he deflected the situation, ensuring it was never spoken of again. This is what they do; they explode and deflect, never to be spoken about again. He never returned the money he took, and any money we gave him was never seen again. But if he gave us money, he would hound us endlessly until he got it back.

By this point in my life, I no longer feared him. I had become numb to him, focused solely on protecting my children. My mindset was, "If he kills me, so be it." I knew he wouldn't, though, he needed me. I was his strength, rock, enabler, and mother, and I excused everything he did. I was deeply trauma-bonded to him, just as he was to me.

After he finally left us for a decade, he never paid child support. He had built his company and put everything in a trust so no one could access his money. I received nothing, no financial help, no contact, nothing. While he travelled the world and bought designer labels for himself, his children went without.

To this day, I don't understand the mentality of an abuser who thinks that making the children suffer will make us come running back. We won't; it only fuels more resentment. The ones genuinely missing out are the children, not us. They punish us through our children, but watching mine go without and sacrificing everything for them became my sole purpose. I knew we would make it through.

I decided to take charge of my life, completing a nail course, working in a salon, and later earning my Diploma in Beauty Therapy. I then became a *TAFE (Technical Education) teacher* and taught beauty therapy. Through it all, my children learned about love, patience, and teamwork through it all.

A decade later, the abuser returned, wanting to be a father again. Given my strong core family values, shaped by generational abuse, unfortunately, I took him back, thinking that this time, the kids wouldn't have to go without, and we could finally be a family now that he had "made it."

When he came back into our lives, I thought things would finally change, and he would help us, especially the kids. But instead, he just watched from the sideline as I continued to work tirelessly to keep my family afloat. Even though we were in a relationship, living apart, I still felt like a single mother struggling to make ends meet.

He never offered to pay for anything unless it benefited him directly.

For example, when we needed to fly to Melbourne for my daughter's graduation, the kids and I had to scrape the money together. He was invited but, as usual, declined yet another critical milestone he missed. Despite knowing we were struggling, he never offered to help, and I didn't ask because it shouldn't have been necessary. If you're my husband, my partner, why should I have to beg for support? He could see the struggle but did nothing.

The same thing happened on my 50th birthday. I was doing everything I could to organise a party within my budget, but again, he didn't offer help. He decided to buy me a pen for my 50th; that's how much effort he put into what would make me happy. He said he bought the pen because he would've wanted that. If I ever borrowed money from him, he would itemise everything and expect me to pay him back, and if I didn't, he would remind me about it. He even gave me a credit card, but every dollar I spent had to be repaid within the month; I couldn't do this, so I never spent on the card. I could never live up to his financial expectations. He once told me how much he admired how hard I worked for the kids, which was supposed to be a compliment. But what I needed was help. He was my partner, the father of my children; he should have been there for us, but he wasn't.

One time, my son asked for $1,500. The abuser lent him the money, but instead of addressing my son directly, he used me as the middleman or his pawn, as he was too weak to face him himself. While my son was grieving the loss of his grandmother and trying to organise her funeral, the abuser had the nerve to demand repayment. He even threatened to file a claim and have my son served at work if the money wasn't returned.

This is what an abuser thrives on, ruining any significant moment, any occasion that doesn't revolve around them. Whether it's a milestone, a celebration, or even a time of grief, they will do whatever it takes to upset you. The abuser didn't care that we were mourning the loss of my mother. If he wasn't the centre of attention, he created chaos to shift the focus back to him.

How were we supposed to grieve my mother when he was pulling this shit on us? Who does that to their child? Instead of making our lives easier, he made everything harder, all to control and destroy moments that should have been about healing and family.

He would spend countless amounts of money on himself but wouldn't give me a cent for groceries. It still shocks me. Who is this person? It became clear that he enjoyed watching me struggle. The more I struggled, the more powerful he felt. The only power he thought he had was financial control. While he sat in his "castle," giving me advice that only led to more bad decisions and financial sacrifices, he watched me reorganise my life so many times for him, and it seemed to please him.

Looking back, I can't shake the feeling that he enjoyed seeing me struggle. He never truly wanted to help. He just wanted to watch me drown, knowing that his money kept him afloat while I fought to stay above water.

Abusers often strip us financially, leaving us powerless to take them to court or fight for what is rightfully ours. In my case, after another decade of being with him, I ended up financially broken once again. I had no choice but to let him take the house, cars, and everything we built together because I didn't have the funds to fight him. He had the money, the resources, and the upper hand. For women like me, it becomes nearly impossible to stand up for us in the legal system, which often favours those with deeper pockets.

One client, for example, fought hard to take her husband to court, but he slowly drained her finances, leaving her with nothing to continue the fight. She's a single mother of six children, receiving no financial support from him. She works tirelessly to put food on the table while trying to pay her solicitor, struggling to get what she deserves as a mother and wife. Every day is a battle between caring for her children and fighting for justice, but as her resources decrease, so does her ability to keep up the fight. She is strong and will keep fighting till the end.

Another client faced a similar struggle. She had dedicated her life to her family, trusting her partner to manage their finances. But when the relationship crumbled, she had no access to their money. He manipulated their financial situation to ensure she couldn't afford legal representation. Like many of us, she had to choose between caring for her children or battling in court. The emotional and financial toll was too significant, leaving her feeling defeated, even though she was rightfully owed support.

This is the cruel cycle we face, being stripped of our financial independence so we can't stand up for ourselves or reclaim what is ours.

I recently discovered that I had initially been left out of the inheritance. The reason? I kept going back to my abuser, and it seemed like a form of punishment for my choices. This revelation brought back the familiar pain of conditional love and rejection, stirring deep wounds within me. However, things have since changed. Since writing this book, my father has reconsidered and now includes me in the inheritance. His support has helped heal some of that old hurt and opened the door to a new chapter in our relationship.

This experience was a powerful reminder of how love, support, and approval can sometimes feel conditional and how transformation and understanding are possible.

It no longer mirrors the dynamic with my abuser—where everything was conditional, and blame always fell on me. Instead, it's become a step towards healing.

Through all this, I've understood that seeking approval from those incapable of offering true, unconditional love will never fill the emptiness inside. You can't change them; you can only change how you respond.

The truth is, I've been heartbroken by someone I once held in high regard, offering love with conditions and punishing me emotionally and financially. Is life fair? No. But I am resilient. The more challenges I face, the stronger I become, and I will always find a way to rise and survive. Now, with the renewed support of my father, I am reminded that relationships can evolve and healing is possible.

The abuser shapes who we become, but while they may hold financial power, they remain with weak souls. We have the power to overcome anything. Money, dear reader, can always be made, but you cannot buy back your sanity or your soul.

I've got you $_{xx}$

My Gift

Today, dear reader, I would like you to engage in a vital exercise after reading about financial abuse.

First, take some time to track instances of financial control by reflecting on and writing down specific moments when your abuser manipulated or restricted your financial independence.

Next, evaluate your current financial situation by identifying areas where you feel dependent or controlled. This self-reflection can help you clarify your circumstances.

Finally, create a financial independence plan by outlining steps to regain control, such as opening a separate bank account, setting aside savings, or seeking financial advice. This process will empower you to take meaningful steps toward your financial freedom.

The Ten W's of Life

__WHO__ you are is what makes you unique. Embrace it and never change for anyone.

__WHAT__ lies ahead is unknown. Be brave enough to step into the mystery.

__WHEN__ life knocks you down, rise stronger and push back harder.

__WHERE__ there are decisions to make, choose the path that leaves you proud, not regretful.

__WHY__ challenges come may be unclear. Trust in your strength and keep moving forward.

__WHILE__ others may doubt you, trust yourself and stay true to your journey.

__WITH__ every setback, remember that growth and resilience come from within.

WORTH *is something you should never forget. Always know your value and never settle for less.*

WISDOM *comes from experiences, both good and bad. Learn, grow, and use it to build a better future.*

WILLPOWER *is what fuels your progress. Stay determined, and let nothing hold you back.*

These ten W's are reminders that you have everything within you to direct YOUR life's path with courage and strength.

Addicted to Hope

> "I release the false hope that binds me.
> I trust my strength; I trust my worth.
> I deserve love, respect, and peace.
> No longer will I wait for a change in
> someone. I am the one who holds the
> power to change my life, and I choose
> freedom, healing, and light."

Definition of Hope: *Hope is a powerful feeling of desire and optimism that things will improve or that a desired outcome will be achieved. A positive and motivating mindset encourages people to look forward to the future with anticipation and confidence.*

Definition of Addiction to Hope: *Addiction to hope can be described as an excessive attachment to the belief that things will inevitably improve despite evidence to the contrary. It can lead individuals to rely on hope as a coping* *mechanism and prevent them from taking realistic actions or seeking help when necessary. While hope is generally positive, an addiction to hope might lead to ignoring warning signs or delaying necessary changes, potentially hindering personal growth or development.*

One of the most complex parts of leaving an abuser is breaking free from the addiction to hope. We often cling to the belief that they will change, that things will improve. This hope keeps us trapped in a cycle of pain and disappointment. Recognising this pattern is the first step towards reclaiming your power and moving towards a future where you are genuinely valued and respected.

'Hope'. It's the one thing we hang onto when everything else feels shattered. In an abusive relationship, hope becomes a lifeline, the belief that things will change, that the person who hurts us will one day become the person we've always wanted them to be. But this hope, while seemingly comforting, is often the very thing that keeps us trapped. It's not just an emotion; it becomes an addiction, an illusion we desperately hold on to, even when the reality in front of us is screaming otherwise.

I was addicted to hope. It was a powerful drug that clouded my judgment, blurred the lines between love and manipulation, and kept me tied to someone who caused me so much pain and heartbreak.

I convinced myself that he would change if I tried harder, loved more, or gave him enough chances. He would stop being the abuser and become the man I wanted him to be. But that's the thing about hope in an abusive relationship: it's based on fantasy, not reality.

Abusers know this. They feed on our hope, using it as a tool of control. They give just enough to keep us hooked, giving us moments of kindness or promises of change when they sense we might leave. These glimpses of what could be an apology show us a little affectionate gesture, buying us gifts, flowers or a promise that things will get better and keep us coming back. We live for those fleeting moments because they confirm our hope, even if they are temporary and followed by more abuse.

Every time I thought he would change, it felt like standing at the edge of a cliff, hoping there was solid ground, but stepping forward only to fall into the same hole of pain. The cycle was always the same; he would hurt me and then apologise, promising that things would be different. For a while, I believed him. I wanted so badly to believe him. But inevitably, the abuse returned, each time worse than the last. I would question myself, blaming myself for not being enough or provoking him. I held onto the hope that next time, it would be different. Does this sound familiar?

Hope became my prison. It kept me in a relationship where I was constantly depleted, devalued, and degraded. But leaving wasn't easy because letting go of hope felt like admitting defeat. It felt like I was giving up on the idea that things could ever get better. And as twisted as it sounds, hope was the only thing keeping me going, even though it kept me stuck.

Hope is often portrayed as something positive that carries us through dark times. But in an abusive relationship, hope is dangerous. It becomes false hope, a hope that is based on lies and empty promises. This kind of hope keeps us from seeing the truth, recognising that the person we're with isn't going to change, and acknowledging that we deserve better.

It's not uncommon for those of us in abusive relationships to confuse the potential of what could be with the reality of what is. We focus on the rare moments of kindness or breadcrumbs and ignore the overwhelming abuse. We imagine a future where things are different, and that vision of a better tomorrow keeps us tied to an unbearable present.

Abusers use this false hope to their advantage. They know exactly when to give just enough to keep us from leaving. Maybe they'll give a heartfelt apology, offer to change, or even go to therapy, seek medications, or, in my case, see priests and become a Christian, anything to keep the illusion of hope alive. But those gestures are fleeting. They are strategies, not signs of real change.

Letting go of hope was one of the hardest things I ever had to do. It meant facing the reality that he wasn't going to change, that I wasn't going to save him, and that no amount of love or patience would transform him into the partner I deserved. It meant accepting that the future I had envisioned with him would never happen. It broke my heart, and I felt shattered for the last time. But as painful as it was, letting go of hope was also liberating, and it felt like I was set free. It allowed me to stop waiting for change that would never come and start focusing on what I could control in my life, my healing, and my future. It was only when I stopped hoping for him to change that I was able to break free from the cycle of abuse.

For so long, I was addicted to hope because it gave me a sense of purpose. It made me feel like I was fighting for something worthwhile. But in reality, I was fighting for an illusion. When I replaced that hope with clarity, I realised that the only thing I should have been fighting for was myself.

Breaking free from the addiction to hope doesn't happen overnight. It's a process of unlearning and relearning. It's about recognising that we deserve more than the breadcrumbs of affection an abuser throws our way.

It's about understanding that no one has the power to change someone else, no matter how much we hope or love them.

Hope should be saved for things that truly have the power to change. In an abusive relationship, that's rarely the case. Moving forward means learning to hope for something real, not this distorted illusion. My dear reader, we should hope for healing, freedom, and a life where you are valued, loved, and respected. That's the kind of hope worth holding onto.

For me, it was through hypnotherapy and Reiki that I found that clarity. These therapies helped me break free from this false hope. Hypnotherapy allowed me to reprogram the subconscious patterns that kept me stuck, while Reiki brought balance and peace back into my life, clearing the emotional blocks I held onto. Once I removed myself from the distorted illusion and embraced the healing, I could finally see the reality of the relationship.

My Gift

Today, my dear reader, I want you to complete this "AS IF" frame technique. This powerful mindset tool helps you become the version of yourself you want to be, even before you feel fully ready.

In an abusive relationship, where your self-worth and confidence may feel stripped away, this technique allows you to imagine and act "as if" you are already empowered, strong, and free from the control of your abuser.

By visualising and behaving like the person who has already overcome the toxic relationship, you begin to shift your mindset, making choices that align with your freedom and healing. This mental practice can help break the cycle of emotional dependency, guiding you to reclaim your strength and take steps toward a life of respect and self-love.

Here's a simple, step-by-step guide for you:

Step 1: Identify Your Desired Outcome

Start by clearly defining what you want to achieve. It could be emotional freedom, confidence, or even healing from past trauma. Write it down. For example, "I want to feel strong and confident in my decisions."

Step 2: Visualize the Future Version of Yourself

Close your eyes and imagine yourself as someone who has already achieved that goal. Picture how you would look, act, and feel. What would you be doing? How would you carry yourself? Engage all your senses to create a vivid image of this future self.

Step 3: Act As If

Now, imagine there is a frame in front of you. Step into it. If you do not want to use the frame, you can begin behaving "as if" you are that person.

Ask yourself:

- *How would I stand, walk, and talk if I were confident?*

- *How would I handle challenges if I were emotionally free? Start incorporating these behaviours into your daily routine, no matter how small the situation.*

Step 4: Align Your Thoughts

Pay attention to your thoughts and mindset. If you start doubting yourself or slipping into old habits, gently remind yourself to think "as if" you are already the person you desire to be. Affirmations such as "I am strong and empowered" can be helpful here.

Step 5: Make Decisions As If

Whenever you're faced with a choice, think about what your future, empowered self would do. Would they stay stuck, or would they move forward? Let this guide your decisions, helping you shift from your current state to the desired one.

Step 6: Reflect on Your Progress

Take some time to reflect at the end of each day or week. How did it feel to act "as if"? Did you notice any shifts in your thoughts, emotions, or behaviour? This reflection helps reinforce the change you're creating.

By regularly practising the "As If" frame, you'll begin to see the transformation take place, moving you closer to your goals with clarity and confidence.

Enjoy my beautiful soul.

I've got you xx

The Power of Denial

"I choose to see clearly, to face the truth with courage. I release the illusion of denial and embrace the strength within me. I deserve honesty, love, and freedom, and I am ready to accept what is real."

***Definition of Denial:** Denial is a psychological defence mechanism where a person refuses to accept reality or the truth of a situation because it is too painful or uncomfortable to confront. By denying the facts, emotions, or consequences, the person protects themselves from the stress, anxiety, or emotional pain that might arise from facing the truth. In the context of abusive relationships, denial often involves minimising or rationalising the* *abuse, convincing oneself that it isn't happening or that it isn't as bad as it seems.*

My dear reader, as you can see from the definition of denial, how it is a powerful force that often keeps us stuck again in abusive relationships. It feels like false hope, leading us to believe things will improve, even when they don't. When we deny the abuse, we make excuses for the abuser's actions, and in doing so, we enable them. It's as if we become their mothers, turning a blind eye to their behaviour just like their mothers may have done.

In my own experience, denial was like wearing rose-coloured glasses. I told myself, "It's not that bad," or "Whatever, it doesn't matter," to avoid the pain of facing the truth. My famous words, "I'm done," I said this multiple times only to go back, hanging onto lies and broken promises. By excusing my abuser's behaviour, I was not only keeping myself safe by shielding myself from immediate pain and heartbreak but also enabling the abuser to continue their harmful actions. My abuser learned that he could get away with anything because he knew I would be back, like a child who tests boundaries and finds ways to manipulate a parent.

When my abuser misbehaved, I found myself constantly apologising for him as if he was a child misbehaving. I would cover for his actions, making excuses for him, trying to smooth things over and explain away their behaviour to others. Like what we do with our children, this is what we do with them. This meant that my abuser could hide behind me, never taking accountability or responsibility for his actions. He relied on me to clean up his mess, to excuse his immaturity, and to take on the consequences of his behaviour, reinforcing his sense of entitlement and lack of growth.

You, dear reader, might find yourself in a similar situation. It's comforting to think that the abuse isn't as bad as it seems or to believe that the abuser will change. Denial protects us from immediate pain but keeps us trapped in a cycle where we constantly enable and excuse their behaviour. We become their enablers, their apologisers, their caretakers, all while they remain immature and irresponsible.

I understand how challenging it can be to confront the truth. It's not easy, and it is quite confronting and heartbreaking, as denial offers a temporary safety shield. However, I've seen firsthand how transformative it can be when individuals like yourself break free from denial.

So, I ask you: How often have you found yourself apologising for your abuser's actions as if they were a child misbehaving? How often have you covered for their behaviour, letting them hide behind you while you deal with the consequences?

It's time to confront the truth and break free from this unhealthy relationship. You deserve to be treated with respect and kindness, and facing reality is the first step towards reclaiming your strength and freedom.

I've got you ₓₓ

My Gift

Today, dear reader, after reading about denial, I encourage you to reflect on how it has shown in your life.

Write down moments when you may have denied or minimised the abusive behaviour in your relationship.

Consider the reasons behind this denial—was it fear, hope for change, or something else?

Next, identify how this denial has impacted your decisions and emotional well-being.

Finally, write a short affirmation to yourself, acknowledging the truth of your situation and affirming your right to see things clearly and take steps toward healing.

This exercise will help you face reality with courage and begin breaking free from denial.

Maybe Syndrome

I remember countless times when I excused his behaviour, thinking that maybe, just maybe, *things would get better*. Like many of us, I blamed myself, believing that if I could change enough, he would finally see me and become the partner I needed. But my beautiful reader, this is a painful illusion. The following are our Maybes, which I am sure you will resonate with.

Maybe if I ignore the red flags, he'll change for me.

Maybe if I move in and care for him, he'll change.

Maybe if he gets over his ex, he'll love me more.

Maybe if we get married, he'll change.

Maybe he'll treat me better if I wear the clothes he wants.

Maybe he'll value me more if I stop speaking to my family.

Maybe if I have a baby, he'll become the man I hoped for.

Maybe if I keep the house spotless, he'll appreciate me.

Maybe if I lose weight, he'll find me more attractive.

Maybe if we have another child, he'll commit to our family.

Maybe if we go on that holiday, things will get better.

Maybe if I change jobs like he suggested, he'll respect me.

Maybe he'll be satisfied if we move away and I give him all my attention.

Maybe if I grow my hair like he prefers, he'll love me more.

Maybe if I wear less makeup, he'll stop criticising me.

Maybe if I come home earlier, he'll be less angry.

Maybe if I cook and serve him, he'll be kinder.

Maybe things will improve when the kids grow up and we're alone.

Maybe if he earns more money, he'll be happier.

Maybe if he finds a job he likes, his mood will change.

Maybe he'll have time for us if he stops working so much.

Maybe if I show him more affection, he'll reciprocate.

Maybe if I give him my body whenever he wants, he'll cherish me.

Maybe he'll be less harsh if I stay silent and avoid arguments.

But my beautiful soul, the truth is, they will never change. Stop waiting for the day when your efforts will be enough because nothing will ever be good enough for them. Please understand this: you are not the problem and cannot fix what is broken within them. Your worth is not tied to their approval or their ability to change. It's time to break free from the cycle of "maybe" and embrace the certainty that you deserve more than this endless waiting.

My Gift

Today, my dear reader, I have an activity for you to do. This will be hard initially as I struggled to learn to love myself again, so be patient. Take small steps.

This activity is designed to help you start loving yourself again by using positive affirmations while looking in the mirror. It's a practice that can boost self-acceptance, healing, and rebuilding self-worth after experiencing abuse.

Choose a time and place where you can be alone without distractions. This could be in your bedroom, bathroom, or any space where you feel safe and comfortable.

Stand or sit in front of the mirror to see your reflection. Take a few deep breaths to centre yourself and release any tension you may be holding.

Look into your eyes. At first, this may feel uncomfortable or bring up strong emotions, especially if acknowledging yourself in this way is new to you. Allow any feelings that come up to the surface without judgment.

Begin by affirming to yourself,

"I love myself."

"I am worthy of love."

"I am strong and beautiful."

Speak slowly and with intention, focusing on the meaning of each word. If saying these affirmations feels difficult, start with something gentler, like, "I am willing to learn to love myself."

Notice how you feel as you speak. You may feel resistance, sadness, or disbelief—this is normal, particularly if you've endured abuse.

Acknowledge these emotions, but continue the practice. This is your space to heal; every moment spent here is a step forward.

Commit to doing this mirror work daily, even for just a few minutes. Over time, you'll see a shift in how you feel about yourself and respond to your reflection.

At the end of each session, recognise the courage it took to face yourself and speak these affirmations. Celebrate even the slightest progress, knowing that each step brings you closer to healing and self-acceptance.

This dear reader is inspired by Louise Hay's mirror work—a gentle yet powerful practice that helps rebuild self-love and self-acceptance. It is especially effective for those who have experienced emotional or physical abuse, guiding them to reconnect with their inner strength and worth.

I've got you xx

Feeling Isolated, Lost and Alone

"I am not alone. I am rebuilding my life with courage and strength. Each step forward brings me closer to a world of genuine connection and true self-worth. I deserve support, love, and a fresh start."

Definition of isolation lost and alone in abusive relationships: Isolation in an abusive relationship is when the abuser systematically cuts you off from friends, family, and any support network, leaving you feeling trapped and disconnected from the outside world. It's as if your world shrinks down to just you and your abuser. Over time, this isolation causes a deep loss, no longer recognising yourself or your worth, and feeling completely alone. Even surrounded by people, you feel invisible, unheard, and misunderstood.

The abuser manipulates this isolation to maintain control, making you believe there's no escape and no one to turn to, heightening your feelings of abandonment and loneliness.

Leaving an abusive relationship can bring about surprising and painful forms of isolation. As a therapist, I have encountered many women who have found that once they take the courageous step to leave, they face rejection from friends and family who may have sided with the abuser or who fear being associated with the situation. This can be particularly devastating, as it often feels like a double betrayal, first by the abuser and then by those you believe would support you.

Reflecting on the profound loneliness that surrounded me during the relationship is heartbreaking. I was isolated from my friends and family, and it wasn't just that they had distanced themselves; I had lost all sense of who I was. I no longer had an identity outside of my abuser. I became consumed by the abuse and the constant drama. My family shut the door on me when I went back to him for the millionth time, and I didn't speak to them for twelve years.

So much time was lost, including the chance to connect with them. Those years are gone, and I can never get them back. The time we missed is a wound that can never fully heal. I was fortunate to spend the last year with my mother before she passed, but the emptiness of all those lost years in between will always feel like a void that can't be filled.

I used to tell my abuser, "I've never felt more alone than I do with you." It's a deep, unique pain to be in a relationship yet feel utterly abandoned. At least when you're alone, you know you're alone—but being with someone and still feeling that isolation cuts deep. It was like a constant ache of unhappiness, a wound that never healed.

As a single mother, I did my best to raise the kids, but the loneliness was overwhelming. I had no partner to lean on, no one to help share the load. The mothers at school turned their backs on me, suspicious that I might try to take their husbands. And those I thought were friends, well, I now call them acquaintances. They believed his lies and saw me as the crazy one while he played the innocent. I constantly felt like I had to justify myself while being cast as the villain. It was exhausting and isolating.

I often thought, "Who would want me? Who would accept me with three kids?" There was no support, no one to turn to. I had to rely on my eldest child to stay home and care for his siblings when I couldn't. There were nights I cried myself to sleep, longing for someone to help. But there was only so much my friends or family could do, and in the end, I was left to deal with the emotional and psychological baggage alone.

The feeling of being lost didn't fade even after leaving the relationship. What do you do when you've been controlled for so long? How do you begin to raise your kids when you have nothing? No money, no direction. The weight of all those questions—Can I do this? Will I make it? —sits on your shoulders while you're expected to stay strong.

This weight, this torment, is something we carry alone. Few truly understand the depth of it.

Starting over after leaving an abusive relationship can feel like one of the hardest things to do. You're not just dealing with the trauma from the relationship but also the emotional fallout from losing friends and support. The loneliness can feel unbearable, and the self-doubt creeps in, making you question whether you can truly rebuild.

But this is also a moment of opportunity—a time to start fresh, to rebuild your life on your terms, surrounded by people who genuinely care about you. It's about rediscovering who you are outside of the abuse and learning to value yourself again.

I know this journey isn't easy because I've lived it. Feelings of isolation, doubt, and being overwhelmed can make you feel like a heavyweight.

Healing requires patience and self-compassion, and I want you to know that you don't have to do it all at once. When loneliness feels too much, the audio in the Limitless Minds Hypno-App guides you, helping you release, process, and rebuild at your own pace.

The isolation you felt during the relationship wasn't about you—it was a tactic to control and diminish you. But now, you're reclaiming your power. Every step you take is toward healing, strength, and self-love; you don't have to walk that path alone.

Remember,

I've got you $_{xx}$

My Gift

Today, dear reader, I want you to listen to the free Rise Above program and listen to the audio "Break the Cycle – Cutting Cords" on the Limitless Minds Hypno-App.

This audio is designed to help you break free from the emotional bonds that keep you trapped in abusive relationships. The aim is to empower you to cut the emotional cord, reclaim your strength, and release the limiting beliefs that have held you back.

Where There is Pain, There is Light

"Growth often requires us to venture into the dark and confront difficult challenges. It's easy to feel lost in these moments but remember that this is part of a greater journey. Embracing these struggles allows you to evolve into a stronger, wiser version of yourself."

Definition of Grief in Toxic Relationships: *Grief in a toxic relationship is the deep emotional pain and sadness that comes from losing the hope, love, or illusion you once had about the relationship. It's not just about mourning the end of the relationship itself but also grieving the loss of the person you thought they were the future you envisioned or the emotional investment you made. This grief can feel* *confusing because, despite the harm caused, there's still a sense of loss over what could have been, making it hard to let go entirely.*

My dear reader, grief comes in many forms when you're in a toxic relationship. We experience grief even while we're still with them, but the most challenging part comes when we finally leave. We go through a rollercoaster of emotions: anger, sadness, fear, hurt, shame, guilt, PTSD, frustration, longing, abandonment, loneliness, and numbness.

We start questioning ourselves: did I make the right decision? Deep down, we know we did, but leaving them feels like detoxing from a drug. It's like our mind, body, and soul are trying to cleanse ourselves of this person, and the trauma bond has us so addicted that it feels unbearable. We're hooked on them like a bad habit.

I remember that feeling so clearly. The addiction was so intense. I left thinking, "Finally, I'm free!" and in that moment, I was. I convinced myself I'd never go back, but I became like the boy who cried wolf. No one truly understands the heartbreak and devastation that hits you like a tornado. It felt like my heart was being torn in two. It physically hurt. I had become so dependent on my abuser that walking away felt like I was losing a part of myself, and each time I left, I lost more and more pieces of who I was.

The attachment is so deep that going through the withdrawal feels like coming off a powerful drug. I kept going back because I was addicted to the highs and the crumbs of affection. That brief moment when everything seemed "good," even if it were just for a day, would pull me back in. It wasn't love; the illusion of love made it so powerful.

You think about them constantly, driving your friends and family crazy because you can't stop talking about them. You miss them, even though you know missing someone who only wanted to break you is wrong. I missed the breadcrumbs, the little bits of attention, the rare moments of affection, the promises that things would change. I held onto the good moments like a lifeline because it felt like all I had left. And that's how it messes with your head and keeps you returning.

You start thinking, Maybe he'll change. What if he changes for someone else? That's not fair. I hate him. I hate myself. Why am I going through this? Why me? Why isn't he hurting like me? How can he move on so quickly, and I can't? Why, why, why? There were so many questions, so many overwhelming thoughts, and so many tears. Gosh, the tears, so many bloody tears. You reach a point where you think there's nothing left to cry, but then a memory surfaces, or you hear something about him, and all those emotions come flooding back. And yep, the tears are back, too.

But eventually, you reach a breaking point. For me, it was when I realised I was losing myself. My soul felt depleted, my worth shattered, and I had hit rock bottom. But through this grief, I had to find a way to heal. I was so broken that I had to rebuild, learn to love myself, and work through each emotion, piece by piece.

My dear reader, I'm sure you resonate with my experience, so let's break down the different emotions we go through:

Anger:

In our anger, we often find the strength to leave finally. It's what pushes us to take that first step, and we deserve a massive round of applause. Anger can be empowering, and it fuels us when we feel weak. Don't you love how sometimes it's also our greatest source of strength?

But then, the anger turns inward. We're furious with ourselves for putting up with their abuse for so long, for going back, for letting them manipulate and control our lives. The rage I felt leaving for the last time wasn't just directed at my abuser. It was towards me. How could I have been so stupid to go back again and again? Through hypnotherapy, I had to release this rage because it consumed me. It was messing with my energy and affecting the people I love.

Sadness:

The sadness we feel is unlike anything else. The heartache, the tears, it's like mourning a death, except they're still alive. It's the kind of hurt that no one understands unless they've been in an abusive relationship. The addiction is so real, and the craving for more of them, more of the toxicity, feels impossible to break. We cry for the person we wanted them to be, for the love we thought we had. It's isolating because when we talk to our friends or family about it, they look at us like we're crazy for missing them. But they don't get it. They don't understand how deep the trauma bond runs.

Fear:

Fear creeps in from all angles. We fear being alone, supporting ourselves, supporting our kids. We fear them coming back, showing up at our door, and breaking the AVO. We fear that, despite everything, we'll return to them. There's also the fear of meeting someone new, of trusting again, and of being vulnerable. And what's worse, we fear love. We fear it so much that we close ourselves off to it.

Anxiety:

Fear naturally leads to anxiety. We're constantly overwhelmed by the trauma that's now stuck on repeat in our heads. We can't sleep, our thoughts race and we're so emotionally sensitive that even the most minor things send us spiralling.

Depression:

Depression takes over, and it feels like you're drowning. The constant crying, the emptiness, the numbness—you can't get out of bed unless you absolutely must or for the kids. Even then, you're just an empty shell going through the motions like Groundhog Day. You're in a room full of people but still completely alone. Sometimes, the pain feels so unbearable that thoughts of not wanting to exist anymore creep in. But you can't let go because of the kids.

Shame:

Shame is huge; well, it was for me. The shame hits you like a tonne of bricks. You feel ashamed for going back so many times, for believing they'd change when everyone else could see the truth. Shame for what you did for them, things you'd never have done in any other situation. Shame for having no money, standing at the checkout, praying your card won't decline, and sometimes having to put groceries back, barely able to feed your kids.

There's shame in being unable to ask for help or having the strength to leave sooner. The most profound shame was not protecting my kids when I should have. I went back, even though I knew he had hurt them. That shame haunted me for so long. I almost lost my children because of it. I look back now and think, "How could you do that?"

Through healing, I've released the weight of that shame. I still remember it, but it no longer holds me hostage.

Guilt:

The guilt weighs heavily on us. We feel guilty for putting our loved ones through the trauma, for letting them witness our pain. We feel guilty for the support they had to give, guilty for leaning on them. The guilt of exposing them to our toxic relationship is hard to bear.

Limiting Beliefs:

These beliefs stick with us as they are generational if we don't break free from them. My beliefs were shaped when I was a child and were only reinforced by the abuse. I carried thoughts like "I'm not good enough," "I'm too fat," "I'm ugly," and "No one will ever love me." These thoughts took over my life. My worth was non-existent. I hated my body, and I didn't love myself. The body dysmorphia made me think I was invisible, unworthy, and broken. We don't realise just how deeply an abusive relationship impacts our mental health. If we don't work to heal these beliefs, we either attract the same kind of person or find someone who carries our emotional baggage.

My dear reader, once you leave your abuser, you need the proper support and help. Take time to heal before stepping into another relationship. Figure out who you are and what you truly want. I know it's hard right now, but I promise you, there's light at the end of the tunnel.

You can get through this. I had PTSD, but hypnotherapy helped me remove the toxic triggers. I didn't forget what happened, but the emotional attachment to those memories was gone. My belief system changed. For the first time, I love myself. I won't let anyone hurt me like that again because now I see the red flags, and I listen to my intuition. That's key: listening to your intuition and not dismissing it.

You are strong and need to know that this isn't the end of your story. There's so much more to you. Find yourself again because you are beautiful and more than enough.

Hypnotherapy and Reiki helped me move through these emotions and release the pain I carried for so long. Let me help you do the same.

I've worked with many clients who, just like me, have struggled with the grief of leaving toxic relationships. Here are two stories of women who found their strength through the HypnoQi program:

Sarah had been in an emotionally and verbally abusive relationship for five years. Each time she tried to leave, she pulled herself back, questioning whether she had made the right choice. The withdrawal from her abuser felt like physical pain. Sarah's grief was so deep that it felt like losing him meant losing herself. What she didn't realise was that she had already lost herself. The fear of being on her own, of facing life alone, was more terrifying than the abuse she endured.

Sarah began to detach through the HypnoQi program and the breakthrough audios on the Limitless Minds Hypno-App. It wasn't easy. Initially, she missed him constantly, driving her friends and family mad with endless conversations about him. But as she worked through the guided sessions, her thoughts of him became less consuming. Slowly, her grief turned into a new strength, and she started to see that her worth wasn't tied to him at all.

Emma's sadness came from a different place. After surviving an abusive marriage, she realised that her relationships had been repeating patterns from her childhood. She was mourning not just her ex but the years of trauma she'd inherited and repeated. She cried for the love she thought she had, the family she dreamed of, and the woman she knew she could have been. Her grief felt never-ending, and each conversation with family or friends made her feel more isolated.

Emma's turning point came when she worked through her limiting beliefs in my HypnoQi program. Her sadness began to lift as she saw how deeply her abuse had shaped her sense of self. By the end of the program, she'd reclaimed her power, learning to love herself in ways she never thought possible.

I am so proud of Sarah, Emma, and the countless women I have helped. Their journeys are unique, but we all end up at the same destination: freedom and empowerment. Letting go of all the negative emotions and triggers is incredibly liberating, and that's why I love my job. It's so rewarding, and I gain great satisfaction from watching these women grow into the amazing, strong individuals they were always meant to be.

I've got you $_{xx}$

My Gift

Today, dear reader, I invite you to take a moment for yourself. A moment to breathe, to reflect, and to begin letting go of the pain that may still linger in your heart.

Heartbreak and grief from abusive relationships leave deep wounds, but healing is possible, and it begins with releasing the emotional ties that keep us bound to the past.

One of the most powerful ways to do this is through the practice of forgiveness—not for others but for one's own peace.

*The **Ho'oponopono Prayer** is a simple yet profound way to begin that journey. It helps you release the burden of resentment, anger, and regret.*

As you say this prayer, you're permitting yourself to heal, to let go, and to welcome peace back into your life.

The Ho'oponopono Prayer for Healing and Forgiveness:

Find a quiet place, settle into your breath, and gently repeat these four lines when you're ready.

Speak them to yourself, to your past, to the emotions or individuals who have hurt you, and to the parts of you still holding onto pain.

I'm sorry.
Please forgive me.
Thank you.
I love you.

Repeat these words softly and with intention as many times as you need. Imagine the emotional cords tying you to the past, loosening and dissolving with each repetition.

Feel your heart becoming lighter as you embrace forgiveness, not just for others, but for yourself.

My dear reader, Forgiveness as Freedom

Forgiveness isn't about excusing what happened to you but about freeing yourself from the emotional chains that keep you stuck. With each repetition of the prayer, you are choosing to move forward with love and compassion—starting with yourself.

You are worthy of peace, dear reader. You are worthy of healing, and most of all, you are worthy of love.

Take this practice with you into your daily life. Use it whenever the pain feels too heavy or when you're ready to release a new layer of the past. In time, you will find that these simple words hold the power to transform your heart and lead you toward greater healing.

Love always, Nicole xx

The Power of Women in Ancient Times

I need to speak to you about this because you must understand something powerful: We were and still are the original superpower. For too long, men have acted as if they hold ultimate control, but deep down, they fear our strength.

Their actions, rooted in insecurity, reflect their attempts to suppress what they know we possess—an undeniable force that they feel inferior to.

Long ago, women were the leaders and held great power in many societies. We were the heart of the family and community, respected for our roles in gathering food, healing, and passing down knowledge. In these early days, we were seen as powerful figures, and many societies traced family lines through the mother, making women central to inheritance and community leadership.

In ancient religions, goddesses were worshipped and admired. Powerful goddesses like Isis in Egypt and Athena in Greece showed that women were seen as divine and strong. These goddesses reflected the high-status women held in their societies.

Over time, things changed, and men began to take over. This shift wasn't because men were better or stronger but because of several societal changes.

When people started farming and living in one place, controlling land and resources became important. Men, who often took on the physical tasks of farming and protecting land, started to gain more control and pushed women out of leadership roles.

As communities grew, conflicts over land and resources increased. Men became warriors and protectors, roles that were seen as more important, giving them more power and status.

New laws and traditions began to favour men. Inheritance and property rights were given to men, and women's roles were reduced to the home. Religious institutions often supported these changes, describing male gods as supreme and sidelining female goddesses.

As men gained power, they felt threatened by women's influence. Historical stories and myths started to portray powerful women as dangerous or evil. This was a way to justify suppressing women and keeping them out of power.

These changes created a system where men held most of the power. Even though society has evolved, the legacy of this male dominance continues to affect us. But it's important to remember that women were once the superpower and still have immense strength and potential.

Understanding this history is crucial for realising that women have always been powerful. Despite the efforts to suppress us, we have the strength and capability to lead and inspire. Remember, we were the original superpower, and we still are. It's time to reclaim our power and continue for equality and respect.

Remember, you are that superpower.

I've got you xx

My Gift

Today, my reader, I want you to listen to the free Rise Above program and listen to the audio "Radiant Goddess" on the Limitless Minds Hypno-App.

This audio is to help you connect with your inner power, wisdom, and strength by envisioning yourself as a radiant goddess.

The Non-Negotiables

1. Teaching a grown man how to love you? That's not love. Love comes naturally—if you have to explain it, it's not real.

2. You should never have to explain your worth. If one man doesn't see it, trust that someone else will. The right person will value you without question.

3. You cannot stop a man from cheating. But know this: his betrayal is not your fault. It never was, and it never will be.

4. Stop accepting the excuse, "This is just who I am." That's not a reason for mistreatment. Never let anyone use that to justify hurting you.

5. A man will always treat you based on his feelings. Pay attention to his actions, not just his words—they reveal everything you need to know.

6. When he shows you his true colours, believe him the first time. Don't make excuses for him, no matter how much it hurts. Trust what you see.

7. A man who truly loves you will move mountains for you. No excuses, no hesitation. Real love shows up without limits.

8. Words mean nothing without action. If he says he loves you, his actions will prove it. If they don't, then his words are empty.

9. Mature men know precisely what they're doing. Don't give second chances to someone who has already disrespected you. You deserve better.

10. You are not asking for too much. You're simply asking the wrong person. You are the complete package—you might be at the wrong doorstep.

11. Love should never feel like a battle for survival. If you find yourself constantly defending your needs or happiness, it's not love—it's control.

12. No relationship should make you feel smaller. If he dims your light, he's afraid of how brightly you can shine. Never let anyone suppress your brilliance.

13. Boundaries are non-negotiable. Anyone who dismisses or crosses your boundaries does not respect you. Stand firm, and never apologise for protecting your peace.

14. Trust your intuition. If something feels off, it likely is. Your instincts are powerful—listen to them.

15. True love empowers. It doesn't deplete. If a relationship drains you more than it nurtures you, it's time to step away.

16. You are not responsible for "fixing" a man or his issues. He must choose to work on himself. Your worth is not defined by how much you sacrifice.

17. Apologizing for your emotions is unnecessary. Your feelings are valid and deserve to be heard without fear or judgment.

18. Happiness is not a gift someone gives you; it's something you cultivate for yourself. A partner should add to your joy, not be the sole source of it.

19. Consistency is key. If he loves you one day and ignores you the next, that's manipulation, not love. Stability is essential.

20. You deserve the love that feels safe, steady, and true. Never settle for anything less than the respect, loyalty, and affection you give freely.

Remember these truths: you deserve real love, respect, and devotion. Never settle for less than what you deserve.

I've got you ₓₓ

'The Let It Go' Theory

I've learned over the years that one of the most powerful tools we have in life is our ability to *let it go*. Whether it's people, situations, or feelings that no longer serve us, releasing the things that weigh us down is the ultimate form of self-respect and healing.

For a long time, I held onto people who hurt me, thinking if I just did more, loved more, or forgave more, things would change.

But dear reader, I understood that the more you hold on, the more you lose yourself.

I realised this: *They wouldn't keep hurting you if they cared.* That's when I decided it was time to let it go. Not because I didn't care anymore but because I started to care more about myself.

So, let it go...

- Let go of the need to be understood by everyone
- Let go of the judgments others throw at you

- Let go of the people who doubt you
- Let go of the need to defend yourself
- Let go of the hurtful words and actions
- Let go of those who make you feel small
- Let go of those who manipulate, mistreat, or disrespect you

When people mistreat you, gossip, or ignore your boundaries, they show you exactly who they are. And that is your key to *let it go*.

They knew what they were doing. They did it anyway. You don't need to chase closure from them. The lack of respect, the lack of care, the lack of honesty—that was the closure.

Let it go because holding on will only weigh you down. You don't have to sit at tables where your name is dragged through the mud when you stand up. You don't have to keep explaining yourself to people who will never see your worth.

You can still love them. You can still care. But sometimes, the kindest thing you can do—for yourself and them—is to love from a distance. Let it go, and *free yourself* from the binds they placed on you.

Remember, your peace, light, and joy are yours to protect. Don't let anyone take that from you. The only thing you can control is your response. So, let go of what you can't control and embrace what you can.

It's not easy. Trust me, I know. There were nights I cried myself to sleep, wondering why people I loved so much could hurt me so deeply. But through the pain, I realised I deserved better.

And so do you.

When you're ready, you'll see that letting go isn't about giving up but rising above. It's about creating space for the people and the life that *will* honour you.

LET IT GO because your peace matters. Your joy matters. *You* matter.

I've got you ₓₓ

Finding Support in Australia – You Are Not Alone

My dear reader, I was fortunate to have the support of my parents and family during my darkest moments. I understand, however, that some of you may not have that same support. That's why I've included a list of the suitable support systems to turn to.

If you're facing domestic violence in Australia, please know that there are many organisations and services available to help. From emergency shelters to legal aid, these resources can guide you in escaping an abusive relationship and starting the journey toward rebuilding your life.

1. National Domestic Violence Helplines

In Australia, national helplines are available 24/7 to provide confidential advice, emotional support, and assistance with safety planning. These services can connect you with local shelters, legal support, and emergency services.

- **1800RESPECT**: A national sexual assault, domestic, and family violence counselling service offering free, confidential support. Call 1800 737 732 or visit 1800respect.org.au
- **Lifeline Australia**: Offers crisis support for anyone experiencing distress, including domestic violence. Call 13 11 14 or visit lifeline.org.au

2. Domestic Violence Charities and Support Services

There are several charities and organisations across Australia dedicated to supporting individuals escaping domestic violence. They provide crisis accommodation, counselling, financial aid, and more.

- **Women's Legal Service (Australia-wide)**: Provides free legal advice and advocacy for women facing domestic violence. Visit wlsa.org.au for state-specific services.
- **Domestic Violence Resource Centre Victoria (DVRCV)**: Provides information, referrals, and resources for survivors of domestic abuse in Victoria. Visit dvrcv.org.au

- **White Ribbon Australia**: Aims to prevent men's violence against women through education and offers resources for men seeking help. Visit whiteribbon.org.au
- **Full Stop Australia**: Specializes in supporting victims of sexual and domestic abuse. Call 1800 385 578 or visit fullstop.org.au

3. Emergency Domestic Violence Refuges and Shelters

If you need to leave your home immediately, domestic violence refuges offer safe accommodation and ongoing support.

- **Safe Steps Family Violence Response Centre (Victoria)**: Offers a 24/7 crisis line for women and children escaping violence and helps find immediate refuge. Call 1800 015 188 or visit safesteps.org.au
- **RizeUp Australia**: Provides practical support to survivors, including relocation services and setting up safe housing. Visit rizeup.com.au
- **Jenny's Place (New South Wales)**: Offers crisis accommodation and transitional housing for women and children escaping domestic violence. Call (02) 4929 6289 or visit jennysplace.org
- **YWCA Australia**: Operates safe houses and transitional housing for women and children across Australia. Visit ywca.org.au

4. Legal Aid and Advocacy

Navigating the legal system after escaping domestic violence can be challenging, especially when children or financial control is involved. Legal aid services in Australia provide free or low-cost legal assistance for those in need.

- **Legal Aid Australia (National)**: Each state and territory offers free legal advice on family law, protection orders, and child custody. Visit legalaid.gov.au for state-specific services.
- **Women's Legal Services Australia**: Offers free legal advice and advocacy specifically for women in domestic violence situations. Visit wlsa.org.au
- **Family Violence Law Help (Australia-wide)**: Offers easy-to-understand legal information and advice on family violence and legal options. Visit familyviolencelaw.gov.au

5. Counselling and Emotional Support

Healing from the emotional and psychological trauma of domestic violence is a long process. Many organisations in Australia offer counselling and emotional support to help survivors recover and rebuild.

- **1800RESPECT (Australia-wide)**: Provides confidential counselling and emotional support for survivors of domestic, family, and sexual violence.

- **Relationships Australia**: Offers counselling services for individuals and families affected by domestic violence. Visit relationships.org.au or call 1300 364 277.

- **Victims Services NSW**: Offers counselling and financial support to victims of domestic violence. Call 1800 633 063 or visit victimsservices.justice.nsw.gov.au

6. Financial Aid and Housing Support

Financial abuse is often a key part of domestic violence. Many organisations offer assistance in securing financial independence and housing support.

- **Centrelink Crisis Payments (Australia-wide)**: Provides financial assistance for those experiencing domestic violence. Contact your local Centrelink office or visit servicesaustralia.gov.au

- **Ask Izzy (Australia-wide)**: A website that connects individuals to housing, financial aid, food services, and more. Visit askizzy.org.au

- **The Salvation Army (Australia-wide)**: Offers financial support, emergency accommodation, and food relief for those escaping domestic violence. Visit salvationarmy.org.au

7. Soulful Healing Hypnotherapy

Soulful Healing Hypnotherapy helps you get back on track after leaving an abusive relationship, using HypnoQi to support your healing journey. You can learn more at www.soulfulhypno.com.au.

8. Limitless Minds Hypnotherapy

Limitless Minds Hypnotherapy is a Hypno-app that has crafted tailored audios to boost your confidence and support your personal growth. All in the comfort of your own home. Find out more at www.limitlessmindshypno.com.

Taking the First Step

Leaving an abusive relationship takes immense strength, but it's essential to know that there is help available every step of the way. Whether you need shelter, legal assistance, or emotional support, these resources ensure you don't face this alone. Reaching out is the first step toward safety, healing, and a new beginning.

I've got you xx

What Does a Healthy Relationship Look Like

"I am deserving of a loving, supportive, and emotionally balanced partner. I welcome a relationship filled with mutual respect, trust, and open communication. My partner is kind and compassionate and values my feelings and boundaries. We grow and thrive together, empowering each other to be our best selves. I am attracting someone who brings peace, joy, and stability. We are a team united by love, respect, and a shared vision for our future. I am ready to receive the love and partnership I deserve."

Definition of a healthy relationship: *A healthy relationship is a balanced, supportive partnership where both individuals feel valued, respected, and emotionally secure. It is built on trust, open communication, and mutual understanding. In a healthy relationship, both partners are comfortable being themselves, express their needs and feelings honestly, and resolve conflicts with patience and respect. They uplift and encourage each other's personal growth while maintaining healthy boundaries. A healthy relationship fosters emotional stability, compassion, and a sense of safety, creating a solid foundation for long-term happiness and connection.*

My dear reader, when we meet someone who is mentally healthy or considered 'normal', they won't love bomb you or consume all your time in a way that leaves you no space to think, unlike an abusive partner. Instead, they will respect your boundaries and allow the relationship to develop naturally, giving you the time and space to see if you genuinely want to be with them. This respect for your boundaries empowers you and keeps you in control of your life and decisions.

I want you to understand and embed this in your mind: if it starts badly, it ends badly. Someone once said, "Why go for the firecrackers when you can go for the fireplace?" This made so much sense!

This phrase completely contrasts temporary excitement and lasting warmth in a relationship. Firecrackers symbolise intense, passionate, and fleeting attraction, flashy and exciting but short-lived. While these relationships may feel thrilling in the moment, they often fizzle out quickly, leaving little behind. Worse, they can trap you in a cycle of abuse, where the highs and lows keep you hooked, but the relationship lacks the safety and stability you genuinely need. In contrast, the fireplace symbolises enduring warmth, comfort, and consistency, enlightening you about the true nature of love.

On the other hand, the fireplace symbolises warmth, comfort, and consistency. It provides steady heat, a sense of security and peace, and the qualities of a healthy, lasting relationship: someone who is dependable, nurturing, and can provide love and support over time.

When it comes to finding the right partner, it's about choosing someone who offers enduring love and stability rather than chasing temporary excitement that may fizzle out. The fireplace is the partner who brings long-term happiness, warmth, and security into your life. This concept reassures you that stability is a worthy pursuit, not a compromise.

Going for someone gentle and kind (the fireplace) will initially feel strange, but I now understand this is what normal looks like. Normal looks like no drama, chaos, blame, broken promises, or emotional rollercoasters. It might seem unfamiliar to you because you've been conditioned to associate intensity and passion (the firecracker) with love when that's not true.

Healthy relationships aren't filled with constant ups and downs. What we've grown used to might make calmness feel boring, but it's not. It's stability, peace, and safety. Imagine that! Feeling safe and secure in a relationship, knowing that you can rely on your partner for peace and comfort.

As you work on yourself, learning to love who you are, standing firm in your own space, setting your standards high, and recognising your worth, you will see this relationship for what it is. We can only embrace the calm of a genuinely loving and supportive relationship when we heal and value ourselves. This empowerment allows you to set the tone for your relationships, ensuring they are healthy and respectful.

When you meet someone and build a healthy relationship, the foundation you create early on is crucial. This foundation sets the tone for how the relationship will evolve and helps you establish trust, respect, and mutual understanding. By understanding this, you can be proactive in setting a solid foundation for your relationships, ensuring they are healthy and fulfilling.

From the beginning, being honest about who you are, what you need, and your boundaries is essential. Now, this doesn't mean rushing to share every detail of your life. Just be transparent and authentic. When both people feel comfortable expressing their true selves without fear of judgment, it builds a foundation of trust.

Respect for each other's boundaries is another crucial element. Early in the relationship, it's essential to recognise each other's space, time, and emotional needs. Now, when I say space, this doesn't mean they don't like you because they didn't answer you immediately or are suffocating you with time. Space is good in a healthy relationship.

Setting boundaries isn't about pushing someone away; it's about establishing healthy limits that allow both partners to feel safe and respected. A partner who respects boundaries shows they value you. Imagine that! Someone valuing you!!!. This sense of safety and respect makes a healthy relationship valuable and fulfilling.

Another aspect of building a healthy foundation is emotional availability. Both partners should be emotionally present and willing to engage deeply with each other. This means, my dear reader, being willing to listen, support, and validate each other's feelings. Emotional availability helps create a safe space where vulnerability is not just accepted but welcomed and met with care. In a healthy relationship, your feelings are not judged or dismissed but understood and cared for.

In the early stages of a relationship, it's important to watch for consistency. A healthy partner shows up reliably, not only in the good times but also during challenging moments. Their actions align with their words, creating a sense of security. When someone is consistent, we know we can rely on them, and this, my dear reader, gains our trust.

However, trust must be paired with caution. Please, I beg you, do not ignore the red flags or dismiss your intuition. I learned this the hard way when an online scammer entered my life, showering me with attention and adoration that masked deeper manipulation. The red flags were there, and I ignored them, convincing myself that my gut feeling was fear. But your instincts are powerful, and they exist to protect you.

Genuine trust is built when you remain aware and check in with yourself, ensuring that your sense of safety is as real as the respect and support shared in the relationship.

Remember, a healthy partnership is not about control or one-sided fulfilment but mutual respect, where both partners support each other's growth and dreams. Don't silence your intuition—listen to it. It's your strongest guide toward genuine and safe love.

Take it slow, my dear reader; take it at a pace that feels right for you. If they don't understand this, they aren't the right for you. Rushing into a relationship too quickly can sometimes prevent a solid foundation from forming. A healthy relationship grows organically, with both partners taking the time to truly understand each other, building intimacy gradually, and respecting the natural progression of connection.

Your partner should be your haven, not another battle to fight. They're meant to provide comfort, support, and unconditional love, not add to your stress, anxiety, or drama. In a healthy relationship, your partner is your rock, confidant, and best friend. They should make you feel seen, heard, and understood, not dismiss your feelings or make you feel like you're walking on eggshells.

A strong relationship is built on trust, respect, and open communication. It's a partnership where both people feel valued and supported. You deserve a partner who allows you to be yourself, free from judgment or rejection. Don't settle for a relationship filled with constant struggle. You deserve someone who will be your ally, support, and forever home.

Emotional stability is essential in a healthy relationship. When life becomes overwhelming, a mature and balanced partner brings calm and strength, creating a safe space where you can be vulnerable and open. This stability allows you to share your feelings without fear of judgment.

A partner should consistently show affection and appreciation. Little acts of kindness help love thrive. Whether it's a thoughtful gesture or words of encouragement, these actions make you feel valued daily.

Conflicts are inevitable but are handled with maturity and patience in a healthy relationship. A partner who approaches disagreements with respect and understanding creates an emotionally safe environment. They don't raise their voice or dismiss your feelings. Instead, they communicate calmly, showing you love and respect even during tough times.

A healthy partner protects your physical safety and prioritises your emotional well-being. They lead with kindness, empathy, and compassion without hidden motives. They grow with you as your teammate and best friend, standing by you through life's ups and downs. They empower you, support your dreams, and encourage you to become the best version of yourself.

In this kind of relationship, fear has no place. Your partner should inspire you, not just with words, but through consistent actions. They keep their promises, showing up fully and remaining true to their word. They make you feel seen, heard, and cherished by spending quality time with you, genuinely listening, and giving you their full attention.

You deserve a relationship where you feel safe, appreciated, and deeply connected. A partner who truly loves you will never hesitate to make sure you feel valued and supported every single day.

My dear reader, finding the right man is about choosing someone who offers enduring love and stability instead of chasing temporary excitement that may fizzle out. The fireplace is the partner who brings long-term happiness, warmth, and security into your life. So, I ask, are you ready for the fireplace? I am!

I've got you $_{xx}$

My Gift

Today, my dear reader, I want to leave you with a manifestation of a healthy relationship. Write it down, and feel free to add anything that speaks to your heart. Once you've done that, place it under your bed.

Then, I invite you to imagine and fully feel yourself in your desired relationship. Visualise being with the partner you want. Feel the love, the connection, and the joy of that relationship. See yourself living it like using the 'As If' frame. See, feel, and hear it; allow yourself to believe it's yours.

Manifestation for a Healthy Relationship

I am ready to welcome a healthy, loving relationship into my life.

I attract a partner who respects me, values my worth, and cherishes me for who I am.

We communicate openly, honestly, and with kindness, building trust and understanding daily.

Our relationship is built on mutual respect, emotional stability, and genuine care. We support each other's dreams and help one another grow.

I am open to receiving peaceful, nurturing, and consistent love.

Together, we create a safe space to be vulnerable, authentic and appreciated.

I release all past fears and doubts, knowing I deserve a relationship filled with love, compassion, and joy.

The love I seek is already on its way to me, and I am ready to embrace it fully.

Breathe, I've got you xx.

You've Got This!

Okay, my dear reader, you are crying or missing the so-called 'love of your life'.

I completely understand. As you now see, I have been in your shoes. I know you are hurting, and yes, your heart is breaking.

But let me ask you?

What have you lost, my dear reader? Think about it.

Now let me tell you what you have lost,

You have lost someone who gave you empty promises,

You have chosen to leave someone who never validated your feelings,

You have chosen to leave someone who made you feel so alone in the relationship,

You have chosen to leave someone who has constantly abused you and put you down,

You have chosen to leave someone who could never take accountability for their actions,

You have chosen to leave someone who gaslit, gave you breadcrumbs, manipulated, and betrayed you.

So, my beautiful soul - yes you! Ask yourself again what you have lost.

Stop overlooking the red flags like I did. We fixate on the breadcrumbs that you think you deserve. We often forget why things didn't work and crave to return to what our subconscious only knows. I know this isn't the road you were supposed to take but listen.

They took you for granted.

They didn't appreciate you or your worth.

They use you as the abuser doesn't know how to love; they only know how to use.

They destroyed your boundaries, friendships, and family.

They made you lose your identity.

Do you know why? Because you are stronger than them, they only try to weaken you because they see your strength.

YOU ARE WORTHY, STRONG, AND DETERMINED TO BREAK THE CYCLE AND CHANGE THE NEXT CHAPTER OF YOUR LIFE!

SO, ASK YOURSELF, WHO LOST WHO?

BRING ON THE NEW CHAPTER IN YOUR LIFE!

YOU'VE GOT THIS!

I'VE GOT YOU!

I GET YOU!

I SEE YOU!

AND I AM SO BLOODY PROUD OF YOU!

LOVE YOU ALWAYS, NICOLE XX

My dear reader, as I bring my story to a close, I want to acknowledge the incredible strength it takes to face the truth—about the abuse, about the trauma, and most importantly, about yourself.

For many years, I lived in denial, wearing the mask of survival while quietly enduring pain that chipped away at my soul. But through this journey, I have learned that healing is possible and that breaking free is not just a dream but a choice we can all make.

The stories I've shared, both mine and those of my clients, reveal the multifaceted nature of abuse—whether it's physical, emotional, financial, or psychological. But they also show the resilience of the human spirit. It's not easy to leave, to stand up and say "enough," but it is possible. I see you. I've been where you are, and I want you to know that light is at the end of the tunnel.

My HypnoQi program, the Limitless Minds Hypno-App, and the techniques I've shared—hypnotherapy, Reiki, and timeline therapy—are not just tools for healing; they are ways to reclaim your power, rise above, and rebuild the life you truly deserve.

This book is not the end of the conversation. It's just the beginning of your journey towards empowerment, freedom, and the life you've been waiting to live. I hope you walk away from these pages feeling seen, heard, and understood, knowing you're never alone in your battle.

Thank you for allowing me to share my truth with you. Remember, when you remove the rose-coloured glasses and see the truth, you also see the beauty of the person you are becoming.

Thank you.
I've got you xx

I want to begin by expressing my deepest gratitude to my father. Your support has meant the world to me, particularly when you helped me find the perfect title for this book. This journey has brought us closer, and I cherish our renewed bond. Your love and guidance have been a pillar of strength, and I am forever thankful.

To my beautiful children, you are my heartbeat and my greatest joy. Your unconditional love, patience, and resilience have been my guiding light through every challenge. Watching you grow into such incredible individuals fills me with immense pride. You've stood by me in my darkest times, and I hope my journey shows you the power of strength, perseverance, and love. I love you more than words can express, and I am beyond proud of the amazing people you've become.

To my mum, who is now in spirit, I feel your presence daily. I know you've been guiding me, helping me find my voice to write this book and speak my truth so I can help others. Your love and wisdom continue to inspire me, and I carry you with me in everything I do.

To my friends, family, and colleagues, thank you from the bottom of my heart. You have been my support system, light in the darkness, and constant encouragement. Even when I felt lost, you reminded me of my worth and helped me rediscover my voice. I am deeply grateful for your unwavering belief in me and the space you held for my healing.

This book and my journey would not have been possible without each of you. Your nurturing hearts and constant support have been my foundation, and I am eternally grateful.

Lastly, thank you to my publishing partner for believing in my story and helping bring this book to life. Your professional support has been invaluable in making this dream a reality.

And to you, the reader, I offer one more gift. When you're ready, I invite you to find the song Unstoppable by Sia. Turn it up, sing it at the top of your lungs, and feel the power, strength and courage within you because you are, without a doubt, unstoppable.

With all my love,
Nicole xx

About the Author: Nicole Logis

Nicole Logis is a dedicated hypnotherapist, Reiki Master, and creator of the HypnoQi Program, which combines hypnotherapy, Reiki, and Time Line Therapy® to help women break free from cycles of trauma. Her personal experiences with overcoming trauma and toxic relationships inspire her work and give her a unique perspective on healing and empowerment.

Nicole's mission is to guide women toward rediscovering their strength, building self-worth, and reclaiming their lives. Her book, I See You, shares her story and insights, offering hope and practical tools for those looking to transform their lives.

Nicole is passionate about connecting with her community and advocating for those who need support. She believes that with the right guidance, every woman can rise, heal, and live a life filled with love and freedom.

Let's Connect

Thank you for joining me on this journey. Your healing and growth mean everything to me, and I'd love to continue supporting you as you move forward. Let's stay connected! You can find me on my website, social media channels, or email.

Here are my social media links where you can follow, reach out, and stay connected:

LinkedIn: Nicole Logis | LinkedIn
TikTok: @soulfulhypno | TikTok
YouTube:www.youtube.com/@Soulfulhealinghypnotherapy
Facebook: https://www.facebook.com/
Instagram: https://www.instagram.com/
Website: https://www.soulfulhypno.com.au/
Email: soulfulhealinghypnosis@gmail.com

Remember, you are never alone in this journey. Reach out, share your story, or simply say hello—I'd be honoured to hear from you.

With love and gratitude,

Nicole xx

www.ingramcontent.com/pod-product-compliance
Lightning Source LLC
Chambersburg PA
CBHW052138070526
44585CB00017B/1884